ESCAPE FROM CULLODEN

by

THE CHEVALIER DE JOHNSTONE

First published in 1820

This edition published by –

THE HOUSE OF EMSLIE
3 Hatton Place
Edinburgh
EH9 1UD

www.emsliesquared.com

ISBN 978-0-9567745-7-6

eBook ISBN 978-0-9567745-8-3

Copyright © in this edition THE HOUSE OF EMSLIE, 2014

Distributed in the United Kingdom by Central Books
99 Wallis Road   London   E9 5LN
Tel: 0208 986 5463   Fax: 0208 533 5821

Cover by M R Design
Set by THE HOUSE OF EMSLIE
Printed and bound by Interpak Books Pietermaritzburg

This publication is dedicated to the memory of

Alick Laidlaw Buchanan-Smith, 1932 - 1991

Publisher's Note

It has been said of storytelling that what matters is not the story, but how you tell it. Equally important is what part of the story to leave out, which may also be true of publishing an old story (provided that the omissions are acknowledged).

This story, *Escape from Culloden*, is taken from James Johnstone's account of his experiences during and after the 1745 Jacobite uprising in Scotland and England, styled as *Memoirs of the Rebellion in 1745 and 1746* by the Chevalier de Johnstone and first published in 1820.

It ought to be clear from what we have omitted from the original text that our interest as publishers lies not so much in the history of the '45 as in the author's account of his escape following the Jacobite defeat at Culloden. What we have left out, then, is everything up to and including the decisive battle of Culloden, save for the retreat of the Highlanders that serves as an introduction to the author's escape over a period of some six months. Subject to what is said below, however, nothing has been omitted from the point where we take up the story.

To the hypothetical reader who might be inclined to complain that the chevalier's account is too subjective and self-serving to be entirely reliable, we advance the following views.

First, if the excitement of this escape story resides anywhere, it is in the author's subjectivity: the passion, the fear, the hardship, the daring, the obstinacy, the anguish, the pain, the philosophising, the relief on finally escaping the shadow of the scaffold – all of these emotions derive their force from the narrator's subjective perception of his predicament. He is moreover outspokenly critical of the conduct of Prince Charles Edward Stuart at various points in his tale, an assessment that is not without interest in relation to the idealised accounts of the exploits, the wanderings and the escape of Bonnie Prince Charlie, who – we are told – acted with 'an unexampled rashness'.

Secondly, we suggest that all history is subjective, to be read with an awareness of its limitations, for what is presented as historical fact can never be entirely accurate in the sense of telling the full story. Like a factual finding by a judge in a court case, it is the fact-finder's best approximation of the truth, based on the probabilities, and it is never infallible. *Escape from Culloden* is no different, having been written many years after the event, although it does have the advantage of being a first-hand account.

Thirdly, it stands to reason that all autobiography is to some extent, in one way or another, self-serving. This does not rob it of value for either the scholarly historian or the ordinary reader delighting in a good story, although autobiographical accounts should always be read with a measure of circumspection, due to their subjectivity.

J M Coetzee, winner of the Nobel Prize for literature, expresses the relationship between storytelling, autobiography and writing with admirable succinctness: 'All autobiography is storytelling, all writing is autobiography'.

The fact is that a good story is a good story, whether or not it is autobiographical. We all enjoy a good story, and if some find it necessary to suspend disbelief, or to discount somewhat the valid literary technique of exaggeration, then so be it. This is *mutatis mutandis* true of every account of historical fact.

Storytelling is probably one of the oldest pastimes known to man. One can imagine cave men and women, after a hard day's hunting or gathering, sitting around the fire exchanging stories. No doubt then, as now, the enjoyment lay in both the telling and the listening. One imagines that the chevalier took pleasure in writing his story (or he would not have done so), but there is no need to speculate as to whether he enjoyed reading. He tells us that Lady Jane Douglas, who sheltered him during his escape, supplied him with 'the best historical authors', and he adds that the taste for reading he then acquired proved subsequently to be 'a great resource against *ennui*'. We express the hope that the chevalier's own story will be similarly enjoyable to his readers, whether or not as a resource against *ennui*.

A word or two on the text. We have worked from the version published in 1958 by the Folio Society, *A Memoir of the 'Forty Five*, the editor of which, Brian Rawson, said the following in his introduction:

> 'Apart from ending with Johnstone's arrival in Holland and not following the uninteresting itinerary of his journey to Paris, the only cuts that have been made in the original text are of minor passages which are either repetitious or irrelevant.'

We have taken the liberty of editing the text somewhat, in order to enhance its readability by twenty-first century readers. In so doing we have tried to achieve an acceptable balance between, on the one hand, simplifying and modernising the language (in any event a translation from the original French manuscript) where it seemed overly cumbersome and ornate, and, on the other hand, preserving the *texture* of the mid-eighteenth century as represented in the *text*. We have also divided the story into chapters, and the chapter headings are our own.

As to the author, he was the son of an Edinburgh merchant who had spent time visiting his two uncles in Russia, no doubt in an attempt to restrain what he himself describes as 'the passionate, impetuous and imprudent character I possessed in common with most only sons'. When he was twenty-six years of age, he joined the Jacobite army at Perth – against the wishes of his father, also a supporter of the house of Stuart – shortly after the raising of the standard at Glenfinnan. He served as *aide-de-camp* to both Lord George Murray and Prince Charles, and he campaigned throughout the '45 until the defeat at Culloden. After his adventurous escape, he joined the French service and fought with the French forces, *inter alia* as *aide-de-camp* to Lieutenant-General Montcalm in Canada. In 1749 he received 2 200 livres of the 40 000 allocated to Jacobite refugees, and in 1761 he retired from the French service with a pension of 300 livres. The following year he was made a knight of the order of Saint-Louis. By 1790 his pension had increased to 1 485 livres, and in 1791 he successfully petitioned the French assembly for 500 livres as compensation for losses sustained during the '45. In addition to *Memoirs of the Rebellion in 1945 and 1946*, he also wrote an account of the French campaign of 1760 in Canada. Ultimately, after the French Revolution, he was reduced to living in penury due to the death of his protectors and *inter alia* the suspension or annulment of his pension. He is thought to have died in round about 1800, prior to the publication of his memoirs.

The chevalier's lasting achievement must be regarded as his account of the '45 and of his protracted escape under the constant threat of execution as a rebel. Not only did he succeed in avoiding the English scaffold, he ensured the survival of his storytelling for the enjoyment of succeeding generations of readers.

T S Emslie
15 March 2014

Contents

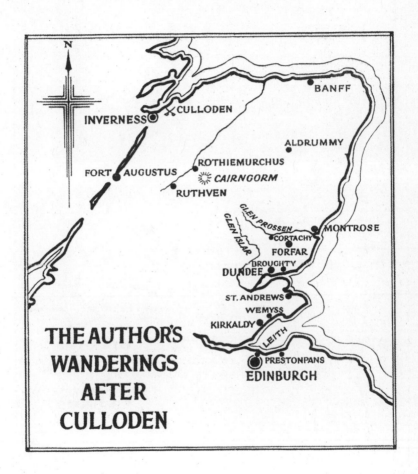

THE AUTHOR'S
WANDERINGS
AFTER
CULLODEN

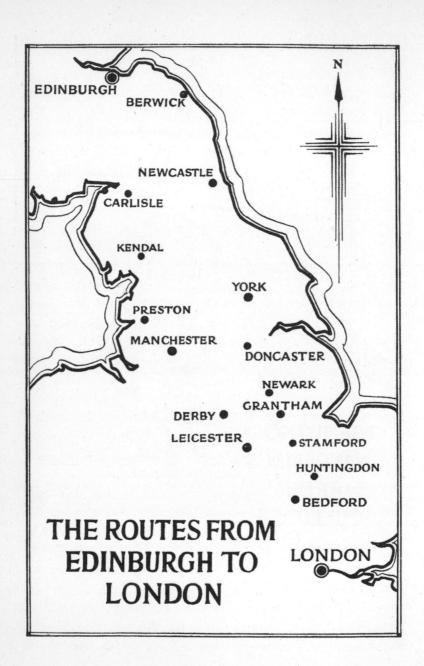

N

EDINBURGH
BERWICK
NEWCASTLE
CARLISLE
KENDAL
YORK
PRESTON
MANCHESTER
DONCASTER
NEWARK
GRANTHAM
DERBY
LEICESTER
STAMFORD
HUNTINGDON
BEDFORD

THE ROUTES FROM EDINBURGH TO LONDON

LONDON

1. Aftermath of Culloden

O n occasions when everything is to be feared, we ought to lay aside fear; when we are surrounded with dangers, no danger ought to alarm us. With the best plans we may fail in our enterprises, but the firmness we display in misfortune is the noblest ornament of virtue. This is the manner in which a Prince who, with an unexampled rashness, had landed in Scotland with only seven men, ought to have conducted himself.

We were masters of the passes between Ruthven and Inverness, which gave us sufficient time to assemble our adherents. The clan of Macpherson of Clunie, consisting of five hundred very brave men, besides many other Highlanders who had not been able to reach Inverness before the battle, joined us at Ruthven. Our numbers increased at every moment, and I am thoroughly convinced that, in the course of eight days, we should have had a more powerful army than ever, capable of re-establishing without delay the state of our affairs, and of avenging the barbarous cruelties of the Duke of Cumberland. But the Prince was inexorable and immovable in his resolution to abandon his enterprise, and to terminate, in this inglorious manner, an expedition the rapid progress of which had fixed the attention of all Europe.

Our separation at Ruthven was truly affecting. We bade one another an eternal *adieu*. No one could say whether the scaffold would not be his fate. The Highlanders gave vent to their grief in wild howlings and lamentations. The tears flowed down their cheeks when they thought that their country was now at the discretion of the Duke of Cumberland, and on the point of being plundered, whilst they and their children would be reduced to slavery and plunged, without resource, into a state of remediless distress.

An incident which took place at Inverness, some days after Culloden, might have proved advantageous to us if the Prince had joined battle at Ruthven. A young gentleman, by the name of Forbes, related to Lord Forbes and a cadet in an English regiment, having abandoned his colours to join the Prince, had the misfortune of being taken prisoner and hanged at Inverness, without any distinction, along with the other deserters. While the body of Forbes was still suspended from the gibbet, a vulgar and brutal English officer plunged a sword into his body, swearing that 'all his countrymen were traitors and rebels like himself'. A Scots officer, hearing the impertinence of this Englishman, immediately drew his sword and demanded satisfaction for the insult done to his country. All the officers took part in the ensuing quarrel, and swords were drawn in every direction. At the same time the soldiers, of their own accord, beat to arms and drew up along the streets, the Scots on one side and the English on the other, beginning a very warm combat with fixed bayonets. The Duke of Cumberland happened to be out of town, but information was immediately conveyed to him. He hastened to the scene of the action before this warfare had made much progress, and he addressed himself immediately to the Scots, whom he endeavoured to mollify by the high compliments he paid them. He told them that whenever he had had the honour of commanding them, he had always experienced their fidelity and attachment to his family, as well as their courage and exemplary conduct, and at length he succeeded in appeasing them.

Thus did Prince Charles begin his enterprise with seven men and abandon it at a moment when he might have been at the head of as many thousands. He preferred to wander up and down the mountains alone, exposed every instant to being taken and put to death by detachments of English troops sent by the Duke of Cumberland to pursue him. The troops followed him closely, often passing nearby, but he evaded them as if by miracle. He declined to place himself at the head of a body of brave and determined men, of whose fidelity and attachment he was secure and all of whom would have shed the last drop of their blood in his defence. Indeed, this was now their only means of saving themselves from the scaffold, and their families from slaughter by a furious, enraged, barbarous soldiery.

The Highlands are full of precipices and passes through mountains, where only one person at a time can proceed and where a thousand men can defend themselves for years against a hundred thousand. As it abounds with horned cattle, of which above a hundred thousand are yearly sold to the English, provisions would not have been wanting. But it would only have been necessary to adopt this partisan warfare as a last resort, for I am morally certain that in the course of ten or twelve days we could have been in a position to return to Inverness and do battle with the Duke of Cumberland on equal terms. When I reflect on this subject, I am always astonished that Lord George Murray and the other clan chiefs did not resolve to carry on this mountain warfare themselves, in their own defence, as nothing can be more certain than what was once said by a celebrated author, namely that in revolt: 'when we draw the sword, we ought to throw away the scabbard'. There is no half-measure. We must conquer or die. This would have spared much of the blood that was afterwards shed on the scaffold in England, and it would have prevented the almost total extermination of the race of Highlanders that has since taken place, whether from the policy of the English government, the emigration of their families to the colonies, or the numerous Highland regiments raised and cut to pieces during the last war.[1]

---

[1] The Seven Years War (1756-1763).

2. A Skulking Prince Fails to Regroup

For several months Prince Charles was hotly pursued by detachments of English troops, and they were frequently so very near to him that he had scarcely quitted a place before they arrived at it. Sometimes he was completely surrounded by them. The Duke of Cumberland never failed to say to the commanders of these detachments at the moment of their departure: 'Take no prisoners. You understand me.'

They had particular instructions to stab the Prince if he fell into their hands, but Divine Wisdom frustrated the atrocious and barbarous designs and pursuits of this sanguinary Duke, whose officers and their detachments – his executioners – inflicted more cruelties on the brave, unfortunate Highlanders than would have been committed by the most ferocious savages in Canada. The generous and heroic action of Mr Roderick Mackenzie contributed greatly to saving the Prince from those bloodthirsty assassins.

Mr Mackenzie, a gentleman of good family in Scotland, had served throughout the expedition in the lifeguards of Prince Charles. He was of the Prince's size and, to those not accustomed to seeing them together, might have seemed to resemble him. Mackenzie happened to be in a cabin with the Prince and two or three others when, all of a sudden, they received information that they were surrounded by detachments of English troops advancing from every point as if they had received positive information that the Prince was in this cabin. The Prince was asleep at this moment, and was woken for the purpose of being informed of his melancholy fate, namely that it was morally impossible for him to save his life. He answered: 'Then we must die like brave men, with swords in our hands.'

'No, my Prince,' replied Mackenzie, 'resources still remain.

I will take your name and face one of these detachments. I know what my fate will be, but while I keep it employed, Your Royal Highness will have time to escape.'

Mackenzie darted forward with fury, sword in hand, against a detachment of fifty men, and, on falling covered with wounds, he exclaimed aloud: 'You know not what you have done! I am your Prince, whom you have killed,' after which he instantly expired. They cut off his head and carried it without delay to the Duke of Cumberland, nobody doubting that it was the head of Prince Charles. Having now, as he thought, obtained the head of the Prince, the great object of his wishes, the barbarous Duke set off for London the next day with Mackenzie's head packed in his post chaise.

The depositions of several persons in London, who affirmed that this was indeed the head of Prince Charles, had the good effect of rendering the English less vigilant and less active in their pursuits. Before that event they had formed a chain from Inverary to Inverness, and the Prince had frequently escaped at great risk, having been obliged to cross and re-cross the chain between their detachments. Mr Morison, his *valet-de-chambre*, was then in the prison of Carlisle, condemned to death, and the government despatched a messenger to suspend the execution of the sentence and bring him to London to declare, under oath, whether this really was the head of Prince Charles. But Mr Morison, having succumbed on the road to a violent fever, accompanied by delirium, was in bed in the messenger's house, where he remained, a prisoner, for fifteen days after his arrival in London. When he began to recover, the head was in such a putrid state that it was considered unnecessary to examine him as it was no longer possible to distinguish any of the features. Mr Morison obtained his pardon and repaired immediately to France, where he still lives.

At length the Prince embarked, on the 17th of September,

on board a vessel which Mr Welsh of Nantes had fitted out and sent to Scotland for the express purpose of saving him. In the month of October he landed at Morlaix, having escaped death a thousand times during the space of five months, and having exposed himself to a thousand times more danger than he would have done if he had acted with courage and perseverance, leading his faithful Highlanders for as long as he could hope to make headway against the English. He should only have resorted to skulking and running about the Highlands without attendants as a last resort, after the passes had been forced and all possibility of opposing the enemy had been destroyed.

But our situation was not desperate. All we can say is that this Prince had embarked on his expedition rashly and without foreseeing the personal dangers to which he was about to expose himself; that in conducting it he had always taken care not to expose his person to the fire of the enemy; and that he abandoned it at a time when he had a thousand times more reason to hope for success than when he had left Paris to undertake it.

The battle of Culloden was lost on the 16th of April due to a series of blunders on our part rather than by virtue of any skilful manoeuvre on the part of the Duke of Cumberland. By terminating the expedition of Prince Charles, this loss prepared a scene of unparalleled horrors for his partisans and precipitated the ruin of many of the most illustrious families in Scotland. The scaffolds of England were, for a long time, daily deluged with the blood of Scottish gentlemen and peers, whose execution served as a spectacle for the amusement of the English populace, naturally of a cruel and barbarous disposition, whilst the confiscation of their estates reduced their families to beggary. Those who had the good luck to make their escape into foreign countries were consoled for the loss of their property by escaping a tragic death at the hands of the executioner. They considered themselves very fortunate withal, for His Most Christian Majesty did not merely grant asylum to the unfortunate Scots who were the victims of their attachment to their legitimate Prince, but set apart a fund of forty thousand livres a year for their subsistence, which was distributed to them in pensions. These pensions have always been regularly paid, but the intention of His Majesty, who destined this fund exclusively for the Scots who were followers of Prince Charles, have not been attended to in its distribution.

3. The Butcher of Cumberland

As soon as the Duke of Cumberland was certain, from the total dispersion of the Highlanders at Ruthven, that he had no reason to fear their re-appearance under arms, he divided his army into different detachments. These were ordered to scour the Highlands in order to pillage the houses and take prisoners. Acting as executioners, they committed the most cruel atrocities, burning castles of the chiefs of clans, violating their wives and daughters, and making it their amusement to hang up those unfortunate Highlanders who happened to fall into their hands.

Orders were at the same time transmitted to all the towns and villages along the two arms of the sea, between Inverness and Edinburgh, to stop any person without a passport from the Duke of Cumberland or the magistrates of Edinburgh. Orders were also sent to all the sea ports of Great Britain, prohibiting all masters of merchant vessels from receiving any person on board without a passport, or from contributing in any manner to the escape of a rebel – a name they had given us since we were the vanquished, whilst we should have been heroes had we succeeded – under pain of high treason, and of being liable to the same punishment as those who had taken up arms. The Duke of Cumberland at the same time detached his cavalry into the Lowlands to seize all who might present themselves without passports to cross the first arm of the sea, with orders to conduct continuous patrols along the coast and to search all the towns and villages in the neighbourhood of the sea.

In consequence of all these arrangements, it was almost impossible to escape the fury of this sanguinary Duke, who, on account of his excesses and cruelties, unheard of among civilised nations, was held in contempt by all respectable persons in England, even by those who were in no manner partisans of the house of Stuart.

He was known ever after as 'the Butcher'.

4. Retreat to Fort Augustus

As for me, my friendship with the unfortunate Macdonald of Scothouse, who was killed at my side during the battle of Culloden, had induced me to advance to the charge with his regiment. We were on the left of our army, at a distance of about twenty paces from the enemy, when the rout began to become general. At almost the same instant that I saw Scothouse fall, to add to the horror of the scene, I perceived all the Highlanders around me turning their backs to fly. I remained for a time motionless, lost in astonishment; then, in a rage, I discharged my blunderbuss and pistols at the enemy, and immediately endeavoured to save myself like the rest. But having charged on foot and in boots, I was so overcome by the marshy ground, the water on which reached to the middle of the leg, that, instead of running, I could scarcely walk. I had left my servant, Robertson, with my horses, on the eminence about six hundred yards behind us, where the Prince had remained during the battle, with orders to keep close to the Prince's servants, that I might easily know where to find my horses in case of need. My first act on turning to retreat was to turn my eyes towards the eminence to discover Robertson, but it was in vain. I saw neither the Prince, nor his servants, nor anyone on horseback. They had all departed, and were already out of sight. I saw nothing but the most appalling of spectacles. The field of battle, from the right to the left of our army, was covered with Highlanders dispersed and flying as fast as they could to save themselves.

Being no longer able to remain on my legs, and with the enemy advancing slowly but redoubling their fire, my mind was agitated and undecided as to whether I should throw away my life or surrender as a prisoner – a thousand times worse than death on the field of battle. All at once I perceived a horse without a rider about thirty paces before me. The idea of still being able to escape gave me fresh strength, and served as a spur to me. I ran and laid hold of the bridle, which was fast in the hand of a man lying on the ground, whom I supposed to be dead. Imagine my surprise when the cowardly poltroon, who was suffering from nothing but fear, dared to remain exposed to the most incessant fire in order to dispute the horse with me at twenty paces from the enemy. All my menaces could not induce him to quit the bridle. Whilst we were disputing, the discharge from a cannon loaded with grapeshot fell at our feet and covered us with mud, without however producing any effect on this singular individual, who obstinately persisted in retaining the horse. Fortunately for me, Finlay Cameron, an officer in Lochiel's regiment, a youth of twenty, six foot tall, and very strong and vigorous, happened to pass near us. I called on him to assist me. 'Ah, Finlay,' I said, 'this fellow will not give me up the horse.' Finlay flew to me like lightening, immediately presented his pistol to the head of this man, and threatened to blow his brains out if he hesitated a moment to let go the bridle. The fellow, who had the appearance of a servant, at length yielded and took to his heels. Having obtained the horse, I attempted to mount him several times, but all my efforts were ineffectual as I was utterly exhausted and had not the strength to do so. I called again on poor Finlay to assist me, although he was already some paces away from me. He returned, took me in his arms with as much ease as if I had been a child, and threw me on the horse like a loaded sack, giving the horse at the same time a heavy blow to make him set off with me. Then, wishing me the good fortune to make my escape, he bounded off like a roe and disappeared from sight. We were hardly more than fifteen or twenty paces from the enemy when he quitted me. As soon as I found myself at a distance of thirty or forty paces,

I set myself aright on the horse, put my feet in the stirrups, and rode off as fast as the wretched animal could carry me.

I was too much indebted to Finlay Cameron not to endeavour continuously to ascertain his fate, but all my enquiries were in vain. His conduct on this occasion was the more noble and generous as I had never had any particular intimacy with him.

There is every probability that I also saved the life of the poltroon who had held the horse, rousing him out of his panic-fear, for in less than two minutes the English army would have passed over him. The cowardice of this man has often furnished me with matter for reflection, and I am thoroughly convinced that for one brave man who perishes in routs, there are ten cowards. The greatness of danger is increased in the eyes of a coward. It blinds him, deprives him of reflection, and renders him incapable of reasoning with himself about his situation. He loses the faculty of thinking and the presence of mind which is critically necessary when facing great danger. Seeing everything through a false medium, his stupor costs him both his honour and his life. In contrast, the man who is truly firm, brave and determined sees all the dangers surrounding him, but his presence of mind enables him to see at the same time the means of extricating himself. Thus if any resource remains, he will turn it to account.

As soon as I was out of range of the dreadful fire of the infantry, I stopped to breathe a little, consider what I should do, and decide which route to follow. During the time when our army had lain at Inverness, I had frequently been on pleasure jaunts to the castle of Mr Grant of Rothiemurchus, situated in the midst of the mountains about six leagues from that town. This worthy man, a delightful companion who was then about fifty years of age, had taken a strong liking to me and had frequently assured me of his friendship, as also had his eldest son, with whom I had been at school, but who was in the service of King George. The father was a partisan of the house of Stuart, but, from motives of prudence, had not openly declared himself. Both he and his vassals had remained neutral during the whole of our expedition. His castle was situated in one of the most beautiful valleys imaginable, a valley equalling anything in the most romantic descriptions of the poets. It was on the banks of a very beautiful river, the Spey, which wound through a plain about a quarter of a league broad and two leagues long. Round this plain the mountains rose behind each other in the form of an amphitheatre, the tops of some of them being covered with wood whilst others were covered with the most beautiful verdure. It seemed as if nature had exhausted herself in forming this charming retreat, for every conceivable blessing of rural beauty had been lavished on it with the utmost profusion. It had enchanted me more than any other place I had ever seen.

During the two months that our army had remained at Inverness on our return from England, I had passed as much of my time as I possibly could at this delightful place, which I had always quitted with regret. I happened to be there when we received information that the Duke of Cumberland had crossed the Spey in the direction of Elgin, and that he was advancing to Inverness. I had immediately set off to join our army, but not without regret at quitting so pleasant a place and the agreeable company of Rothiemurchus, a most amiable, mild, honourable and accomplished gentleman, possessed of an even temper, great natural gaiety and wit, and a great fund of good sense and judgment. On taking leave of him, he clasped me in his arms, embraced me tenderly with tears in his eyes, and said: 'My dear boy, should your affairs take an unfortunate turn, which may be the case, come straight to my house as a hiding place, and I will answer for your safety with my life.'

His mountains being, in reality, a secure asylum against all the researches of the English troops, I resolved, without hesitation, to take the road to Rothiemurchus, which was on our right from the field of battle. I had not advanced a hundred paces, however, when I saw a body of English cavalry before me, barring the way. I turned back, taking the road to Inverness until I saw from an eminence that the bulk of our army was hastening in that direction, from which I judged that the principal pursuit of the enemy would be along that way. I therefore quitted that road also, and went straight across the fields without any design other than getting as far as possible from the enemy.

On reaching the banks of the river Ness, a quarter of a league higher up than the town of Inverness and almost the same distance from the field of the battle, I stopped to consider the route I should take, as the enemy cavalry on the road to Rothiemurchus had totally disconcerted me. Agitated, and tormented by my uncertainty, having never been in this part of the mountains, I suddenly heard the sound of brisk fire, lasting a good few minutes, from the town. As in misfortune one's imagination is often filled with delusive hopes, I at first thought it might emanate from the Highlanders, defending the town against the English, and I bitterly regretted having quitted the Inverness road. I recollected that there was a footpath leading to the town by the banks of the river along which I had several times engaged in fishing excursions. Having discovered this road, I immediately took it without giving myself time to reflect that the place was not capable of any defence, surrounded as it was by a wall suitable only for an enclosure. I had not gone a hundred paces when I met a Highlander fleeing the town, who assured me that the English had entered Inverness without meeting any resistance. He told me that the whole of the road from the field of battle to

Inverness was littered with corpses, and that the streets of the town were likewise covered with dead as the bridge at the end of the principal street had been obstructed by the fugitives. I was not sorry to find that my first conjectures were, alas, all too accurate, for, had I followed the road to the town, I should have numbered amongst the dead. I returned then, my heart more oppressed than ever and plunged into the deepest grief.

As all my hopes had vanished, I thought only of removing myself as far as possible from that fatal spot. The Highlander informed me that he was going to Fort Augustus, a small place about thirty miles from Inverness, which our army had demolished some time before, so I took the high road under his guidance and proposed that we proceed there together.

We reached Fort Augustus at about midnight without finding a single hut along the way. I alighted at a very small cottage which had the name of a public house. The landlady had nothing to offer me but a piece of oaten bread and some whisky, with a little hay for my horse. The hay for my horse pleased me the most for, although I had tasted nothing during the past twenty-four hours, the terrible vicissitudes I had experienced, in the most cruel and unfortunate day I had yet known, had completely taken from me all appetite or disposition to eat. Being utterly fatigued in mind and body, I slept for two or three hours on a seat beside a fire, for there were no beds in the house.

5. Gaiety and Gloom at Ruthven

I had throughout looked upon Rothiemurchus as my only salvation, but his castle was south of Inverness whereas, being now at Fort Augustus, I was further away than when I had left the field of battle. I therefore quitted the cabin before daybreak, having found another guide who conducted me to Garviemore, twelve miles south of Fort Augustus. The next day I proceeded to Ruthven in Badenoch, a mere two leagues distant from Rothiemurchus.

Hitherto I had fallen in with no person who could give me any news, and I was therefore agreeably surprised on finding that this little town had, by chance, become the rendezvous of a significant part of our army, for no place had been nominated as a rallying-point in the event of defeat. In an instant I was surrounded by a number of my companions who eagerly announced that a great part of our army was at Ruthven and in its neighbourhood, and that the Highlanders were in the best disposition for taking their revenge, expecting to be led into battle and awaiting with impatience the return of an *aide-de-camp* whom Lord George Murray had sent to the Prince to receive orders. I never felt more intense joy than on this occasion, and can only compare my emotion to that of a sick person who, after languishing for a long time, suddenly finds himself restored to a state of perfect health. Having learned that there was no accommodation at Ruthven, the greater part of our people being obliged to sleep in the fields, I did not alight from my horse but, after making every possible enquiry after Finlay Cameron, to express my gratitude to him, without obtaining any information as to what had befallen him, I made my way to Killihuntly, about a quarter of a league from Ruthven.

When our army retreated to the north of Scotland, I had

stopped at the mansion of Mr Gordon of Killihuntly, passing several days most agreeably and receiving many civilities. This amiable family now received me in the friendliest manner, and I found Lord and Lady Ogilvie there with several other friends. As I had tasted nothing for forty hours but a crust of oaten bread and some whisky, I did great honour to the good cheer of the lady of the house. And as I had been a stranger to a bed since we had left Inverness to meet the enemy, I immediately went to rest with a mind at ease, and slept for eighteen hours without waking. The next day, after dinner, I went to Ruthven, but the *aide-de-camp* had not yet returned and there was nothing to be learned there, so I returned to sleep at Killihuntly. I was delighted to see the gaiety of the Highlanders, who seemed to have returned from a ball rather than from defeat.

I passed the night impatiently and with uneasiness, and rose early the next morning, proceeding again to Ruthven. On entering the place, I was immediately struck by the gloom and melancholy etched on the countenance of every person I met. I soon learned that it was fully justified. The first officer I fell in with told me that the *aide-de-camp* had returned, and that the only answer he had brought from the Prince was: 'Let every man seek the means of escape as best he can', a sad and heartbreaking answer for the brave men who had sacrificed everything for him.

I immediately returned to Killihuntly with a sad and heavy heart, to take leave of my friends and thank them for their civilities. The lady offered me asylum in the fastness of their mountains, which are very solitary and difficult of access. She told me she would cause a hut to be constructed for me in the most remote location, where she would take care to lay in every kind of provision, that I should not want for books, and that she would give me a flock of seven or eight sheep to take care of. She added that, the proposed place being a mile distant from the castle on the banks of a stream abounding in trout, I might amuse myself by fishing, and she would regularly take a walk in that direction to visit her shepherd.

This prospect pleased me very much at first, for my misfortunes had suddenly metamorphosed me into a philosopher and I should have consented to pass the whole of the rest of my days in solitude if my mind could at once be easy and free from anxiety. Besides, it was now the beginning of summer and the natural beauties of the country, the waterfalls, the mountain glens, the rivers, lakes and woods, in short everything, was irresistibly attractive. Indeed, the magnificence and grandeur which nature there displayed could hardly fail to produce a strong impression on the most insensible of minds. A thousand wild graces eclipsed any beauty of art. A poet or a painter might have selected such a spot as an inspired abode, calculated to give birth to those ideas which never can be effaced from the mind of man.

Besides, the amiable society of Mr and Mrs Gordon, who then showed so much friendship towards me, led me to think that I could not do better. But before coming to a decision I wished to see my good friend Rothicmurchus and consult with him as to the possibility of finding a means of embarking for a foreign country, that I might not remain eternally between life and death. After dinner I went, therefore, to Rothiemurchus, which is situated at the other extremity of this beautiful valley, nearly two leagues from Killihuntly, but the father was not at home. He had gone to Inverness as soon as he heard the news of our defeat, to pay court to the Duke of Cumberland, more from fear of the mischief this barbarous Duke might do him than from any attachment to the house of Hanover. I found his son there, however, and also Gordon of Park, lieutenant-colonel of Lord Lewis Gordon, Gordon of

Cobairdie, his brother, and Gordon of Abachie.

Young Rothiemurchus strenuously advised me to surrender myself a prisoner to the Duke of Cumberland on account of the difficulty, or rather the impossibility, of effecting an escape, alleging at the same time that those who surrendered immediately could hardly fail to obtain their pardon. He added that he had just returned from Inverness, whither he had conducted Lord Balmerino, who had followed his advice and surrendered. I by no means relished this perfidious advice of my old schoolfellow, whose character was very different from that of his father. I replied that I trembled at the very idea of finding myself ironed in a dungeon, that I would preserve my liberty for as long as I could, and that if and when I could no longer avoid falling into the hands of the Duke of Cumberland, he might then do with me as he pleased. I should then meet my fate with resignation. It warrants mention that the unfortunate Lord Balmerino was beheaded in London during the time I was concealed there, and died with an astonishing constancy and bravery, worthy of an ancient Roman.

The servant of Rothiemurchus told us that, having gone over the field of battle, there appeared to be as many English as Highlanders among the dead, and it gave us some consolation to think that they had not obtained an easy victory.

Gordon of Park, his brother and Abachie, having resolved to go to their estates in Banffshire, about ten or twelve leagues to the south of Rothiemurchus, proposed that I should accompany them. I consented the more willingly as my brother-in-law, Rollo, now a peer of Scotland, was settled in the sea port of Banff, where he had the inspection of merchant ships in virtue of an office lately obtained by him from the government. I hoped, through his means, to find an opportunity of escaping abroad. Thus situated, I abandoned without difficulty the project of becoming a shepherd to Mrs Gordon, which would have kept me too long in a state of uncertainty as to my fate. Besides, I was a stranger in the Highlands and wholly unacquainted with the local tongue, and so I was more inclined to place myself under the auspices of Gordon of Park.

After staying at Rothiemurchus for two or three days, we all set off and, having proceeded some miles, slept at the house of one of their friends near a mountain called Cairngorm.

These gentlemen yielded to the entreaties of their friend to stay a day at his house, which displeased me not at all. Forgetting our disasters for a moment, I rose at an early hour and flew immediately to the mountains among the herdsmen, where I found some pretty and beautiful topazes, two of which, sufficiently large to serve as seals, I later presented to the Duke of York[1] in Paris. When I returned to dinner, my friends, seeing me enter with a large bag of flints, erupted in a fit of loud laughter. Gordon of Park exhorted me very seriously to think of saving myself from the gallows rather than collecting pebbles. My mind was, however, as much occupied as theirs with our unfortunate situation, and the scaffold was as deeply imprinted on my imagination as it was on theirs. I knew at the same time, however, that the possession of a few stones would not hasten my destiny if my fate were to be hanged, whilst the search for them dissipated for a moment the fears that consumed my companions in misfortune.

[1] Prince Charles's brother.

6. Rebuffed in Banff

We reached Banffshire on the fourth day after our departure from Rothiemurchus, and it became necessary for us to separate, for the people there were all Calvinists and declared enemies of the house of Stuart. We had lodged the preceding night at the house of a Mr Stuart, a Presbyterian minister, but a very respectable man and secretly in the interest of Prince Charles. On rising in the morning, I exchanged with his servant my laced Highland dress for an old labourer's dress, quite ragged and exhaling a pestilential odour. This, according to all appearances, had for several years been used only when he cleaned the stables of his master, for it smelt so strongly of dung as to seem absolutely infectious at a distance. Having made a complete exchange with him, to the extent even of our shoes and stockings, each of us found our advantage in it – particularly myself, as these rags were to contribute to save my life. Thus metamorphosed, we took leave of each other, each man taking a different road. Gordon of Park advised me to spend the night at his castle of Park, and I accepted his offer the more readily as, being only a league and a half from Banff, it was conveniently situated for an interview with my brother-in-law, Rollo. I was not, however, without fear of meeting some detachment sent out to surprise Mr Gordon, who was closely related to the Duke of Gordon, and which might have made me a prisoner in his stead. I found in this mansion his cousin, Mrs Menzie, a very amiable, sprightly and sensible lady, with whom I had passed some time most delightfully at the house of Mr Duff, provost of Banff, whose family was one of the most agreeable and respectable I had known in the whole course of my life, and whose charming society I had quitted with the greatest possible regret, to rejoin our army at Inverness.

Mrs Menzie told me that there were four hundred English soldiers in the town of Banff, and strongly advised me not to expose myself by going there. However, as all my hopes of escaping to a foreign country rested on an interview with my brother-in-law, I was determined to go, and set off on foot at about nine o'clock the following evening, leaving my horse behind until I returned. On entering the town, I passed a number of soldiers, who paid no attention whatsoever to me, a very favourable omen for the success of my disguise as a beggar. Indeed, my clothes were so bad that the lowliest peasant would have been ashamed to wear them. My blood boiled in my veins at the sight of the soldiers, whom I considered the authors of all the anxiety and distress I had begun to feel, and I had difficulty preventing myself from casting looks expressive of rage and indignation at them. However, I proceeded on my way, earnestly invoking the Supreme Being to favour us with a single opportunity of taking vengeance on them for their cruelties at Culloden. I would then be able to die tranquil and satisfied.

I went straight to the house of Mr Duff, where I had been so agreeably entertained a short time before. He was secretly a partisan of the Prince, but – being prudent and discreet – he avowed his principles only to his particular friends. He was one of the most amiable men in the world, endowed with every good quality and possessing true merit. He was of an equal mind, a gay and sprightly disposition, and he had ample good sense, judgment, talent and discernment. Mrs Duff resembled her husband in everything, and their two daughters, the youngest of whom was a great beauty, were exact copies of their father and mother. There was a uniformity of thinking in Mr Duff's household, and I shall regret the loss of their delightful company for as long as I shall live. As the maid-servant who opened the door did not know me, on account of my disguise, I told her I was the bearer of a letter for her master which I was charged to deliver into his hands only, and I asked her to inform him accordingly. Mr Duff came downstairs and, at first, failed to recognise me, just as his maid had done. Having fixed his eyes on me for some moments, however, his surprise when he did recognise me was accompanied by a flood of tears. He vehemently exhorted the maid to fidelity and secrecy. As Mrs Duff and her daughters were abed, he conducted me into a room and immediately sent his maid in quest of my brother-in-law. The latter happened to be away from home, however, and could not be found, notwithstanding every search that was made for him. As the proximity of the soldiers was too alarming to permit any tranquillity, it had not been my intention to sleep in Banff. I had anticipated seeing my brother-in-law right away to find out whether I had anything to hope for from his services at a moment so critical for me. I therefore resolved to leave Banff before daylight and to return to Mr Gordon's house, and when I went to bed after Mr Duff had retired at one o'clock in the morning, I was unable to close an eye.

I rose before dawn and put on my rags. Whilst I was seated in an armchair, my eyes fixed on the fire – pensive, melancholy and absorbed in a train of reflections suggested in abundance by my predicament – the maid-servant suddenly entered my chamber and told me I was undone, as the courtyard was filled with soldiers come to seize me. Less important intelligence would have been enough to rouse me out of my reverie, and I immediately flew to the window and saw the soldiers. Having thus obtained ocular confirmation of my misfortune, I returned to my chair perfectly resigned and considered myself a man about to end his days. I imagined that the maid must have betrayed me, having possibly some soldier for her sweetheart, a common enough occurrence. One feeble ray of hope remained, to open a passage for myself through the soldiers with a pistol in each hand, and I kept my eye steadfastly on the door of my chamber, ready to spring on the soldiers like a lion should they enter. A desperate and melancholy resource indeed! I had little hope of success, but there was no alternative.

Having thus passed about a quarter of an hour in the most violent agitation, the door of my chamber at length opened, and I sprang forward with precipitation to the attack. Imagine my surprise when, in place of the soldiers, I saw the beautiful and adorable Miss Duff, the younger, burst in like an out of breath guardian angel, telling me to relax. The disturbance had been occasioned by a group of soldiers fighting amongst themselves, and they had entered the courtyard to avoid observation by their officers. After settling their quarrel by way of a boxing match, they had disappeared *en masse*.

Miss Duff the younger was very beautiful and only eighteen years old. I seized her in my arms, pressed her to my bosom, and gave her, with the best will in the world, a thousand tender kisses. In an instant the whole family was in my room to congratulate me on my happy deliverance, for the noise of the soldiers had woken every person in the house although it was hardly six o'clock in the morning. Fully convinced of the sincere friendship and esteem of this respectable family, my greatest unease during this adventure was lest, from their excessive anxiety for me, some of them should have innocently betrayed me. Mr Duff was the only person on whose coolness and presence of mind I felt I could fully rely.

My brother-in-law called on me a few minutes after the alarm was over. He made many protestations of friendship but at the same time excused himself from contributing in any manner to assist me in procuring a passage for some foreign country. He did so on the ground that all the vessels in Banff were strictly searched by different officers of government before their departure, and he strongly advised me to return to the Highlands as the only course open to me. I own that I felt indignant at his conduct, the more so as he was under numberless obligations to me, and I replied that I required his assistance, not his advice. He took his departure after remaining a quarter of an hour with me, during which time he seemed as if on thorns, and from that moment to this I have neither seen nor heard from him. He knew all the masters of trading ships at Banff and, had he been disposed to help me, he could certainly have found someone of their number to take me on board disguised as a sailor, which would have saved me from the infinity of troubles and sufferings I encountered before effecting my escape. But he would not take the slightest risk for a brother-in-law who on all occasions had given him the most essential proofs of his friendship. He was of such a character that I do not believe he would have put himself to any inconvenience for his own father, or for any other human being on the face of the earth.

Adversity is the touchstone of man, and I have learned from mine how little reliance ought to be placed on friendship in general. All those from whom I hoped for assistance in my misfortuncs threw off the mask and displayed nothing but falsehood and dissimulation, and it was only those from whom I did not expect any services who acted as sincere friends. From having been deceived my whole life, experience has at length taught me to know mankind.

Having passed the whole day at Mr Duff's in as agreeable a manner as was compatible with my predicament, I took my final leave of that amiable family at about nine o'clock in the evening, to return to the castle of Gordon of Park. The tears at our parting were abundant and reciprocal. I spent the night, without going to bed, in conversation with Mrs Menzie, not without fear of a visit from some detachment sent in pursuit of Mr Gordon, for the mistake would have been disastrous for me. After lengthy discussion with this lady as to what I should do, I decided at last to head for the Lowlands, and to try by every means to reach Edinburgh. There I could receive help from my relations and friends, or perish in the attempt, whereas in the Highlands I knew no one but those plunged into the same fugitive despair as me. Accordingly I decided to regard myself thenceforth as a lost man, against whom the odds were a thousand to one that he would end his days on the scaffold, but with one chance still remaining. I would abandon myself wholly to Providence and rely on chance rather than any certain resource. I resolved to preserve, on all occasions, the coolness and presence of mind that were absolutely necessary to extricate me from the troublesome encounters to which I would be exposed, the coolness and presence of mind that would enable me to seize any favourable opportunity that might come my way. Such were my convictions, and I was determined to execute them rigorously and to contemplate nothing that might divert me from my purpose.

Mrs Menzie did everything in her power to make me change my plan. She mentioned the insuperable difficulties I would encounter at every turn; the hostile counties I would have to pass through, where all the peasants were fanatical Calvinists who assembled, with ministers of religion at their head, on expeditions to take as prisoners such unfortunate gentlemen as had made their escape from the Highlands; the pursuit of the soldiers; the great distance from the castle of Park to Edinburgh; and the impossibility of crossing the two arms of the sea without a passport from the government, as English cavalry were constantly patrolling the shore and searching the different villages to examine and arrest all persons without passports. But nothing could shake my determination to proceed south.

7. Roasted Fowls and Oatmeal

At about five o'clock in the morning, I took my leave of Mrs Menzie, who gave me a letter of recommendation to Mr Gordon of Kildrummy. He was one of her relations who lived about twelve miles from the castle of Park, and she gave me a servant to accompany me as a guide, whom I could send back once we were in sight of his mansion.

On asking for Mr Gordon, I was told that he had just gone out but that he would be back for dinner. The servant added, in a tone of indifference, that if I were cold I could in the meantime go into the kitchen and warm myself. As it was very cold I accepted this offer and entered the kitchen, where I found a number of servants assembled around the fire. Believing themselves to be of a class above mine, they allowed me to remain standing a long time before inviting me to sit down and join them, which I did very respectfully. They embarrassed me greatly by their incessant questions. One lackey asked me if I had been long in the service of Mrs Menzie. I replied, with an air of the utmost humility and submission, that I had not yet been two months in her service. A chambermaid whispered to a lackey, sufficiently loudly for me to hear, that Mrs Menzie ought to be ashamed to send so shabbily dressed a servant with commissions for her master. Their jargon, stupidity and impertinence wearied me to death, and irritated me for two long hours until Mr Gordon eventually arrived.

I handed him Mrs Menzie's letter, in front of his servants, and followed him to his apartment. As soon as we were alone, I told him who I was and begged him to procure me a guide to conduct me to the first arm of the sea, as I was unacquainted with the country. He appeared greatly affected by my predicament, showed me every possible kindness, and immediately sent a servant with an order to one of his gamekeepers to procure me a guide to his estate of Kildrummy, sixteen miles distant. While we were awaiting the return of the servant, he contrived to bring some provisions into the room. I ate these without any appetite and purely as a precaution, not knowing whether I should get any supper at Kildrummy. When the guide arrived, I took my leave of Mr Gordon and reached the village of Kildrummy at an early hour.

As there were only a few cottages there, I passed the night in one that went by the name of a public house, and slept very uncomfortably on a bed of straw. To make amends for my rough bed, the landlady gave me an excellent young fowl for supper, and surprised me the next morning by asking only three pence for my supper and bed. This public house was an extraordinary one, for it contained no liquor of any description. Nevertheless this outset gave me great pleasure, for I would at least not have to cope with hunger in addition to other sufferings on my journey south. Mr Gordon had sent an order to Kildrummy to furnish me with a guide to Cortachie, a village belonging to Lord Ogilvie, at the foot of the mountains I had kept close by since my departure from Banff. Before leaving, I ordered my landlady to roast another fowl for me and put it in my pocket by way of precaution, for I was uncertain whether I should find anything to eat in the course of the day. When I gave a sixpence to this good woman, she seemed as pleased as I myself was. These fine people had very little money, but they had little need of it as they possessed the necessaries of life in abundance.

As soon as my guide had conducted me sufficiently far on the road that I could not go wrong, I sent him back, and I reached Cortachie in the evening. In traversing the moor of Glenelion,[1] I had wanted very much to encounter the minister

[1] Probably Glenisla.

of that parish, a sanguinary wretch who made a practice of scouring the moor daily with a pistol concealed under his greatcoat, which he instantly presented to the breasts of any of our unfortunate gentlemen he encountered, in order to take them prisoners.

This iniquitous interpreter of the word of God considered it a holy undertaking to bring his fellow creatures to the scaffold, and he caused the death of several whom he had thus taken by surprise. Mrs Menzie had cautioned me to be on my guard, but I was not afraid of him as I always had with me my English pistols, of excellent workmanship, loaded and primed, one in each breeches pocket. Indeed I wanted nothing so much as to come across him for the good of my companions in misfortune, being confident that I would have given a good account of myself in an engagement with pistols, for I have all my life remarked that an unfeeling, barbarous and cruel man is never brave. But the punishment of this inhuman monster was reserved for Mr Gordon of Abachie.

When we had separated, four days after our departure from Rothiemurchus, Abachie had resolved to go to his own castle. The minister of Glenelion, having been informed of his return, put himself at the head of an armed body of his parishioners, true disciples of such a pastor, and proceeded with them to the castle of Abachie in order to take Mr Gordon prisoner. The latter was able to save himself only by jumping out of a window in his nightshirt. As we seldom pardon a treacherous attempt on our life, Mr Gordon assembled a dozen of his vassals some days later, set out with them at night, and contrived to obtain entrance to the house of this fanatical minister. Having found him in bed, they immediately performed on him the operation Abelard formerly underwent, and carried off his manhood as trophies, assuring him at the same time that if he repeated his nightly excursions with his parishioners, they would pay him a second visit which would cost him his life. In this adventure his wife alone was to be pitied. As for himself, his punishment was not as unfortunate as the death on the scaffold he had intended for Mr Gordon of Abachie, and it was to be hoped that this chastisement cured him of his lust for inhuman excursions.

As most of the vassals of Lord Ogilvie had been in the army of Prince Charles, I ran no risk in applying to the people of the first house I came to in Cortachie.[1] Having entered a public house and informed the landlady that I belonged to the army of the Prince, she immediately told me that two of our gentlemen were concealed in Glen-Prossen, a large ravine between two mountains, at the bottom of which there was a small rivulet. This glen lay at the foot of the mountains and was a most picturesque and retired spot. Having enquired my way to them and received the necessary directions, I proceeded immediately to the house of a peasant named Samuel, who lived at the head of the glen about half a league from Cortachie, and there I found the two gentlemen in question. They were Messrs Brown and Gordon, officers in the service of France who had escaped from Carlisle after the capitulation. They were very glad to see me, and strongly urged me not to attempt proceeding any further south, where I should infallibly be taken. They had received information that all the towns and villages on the banks of the first arm of the sea, the Firth of Tay, were searched with the utmost strictness and vigilance by patrols of cavalry. These were constantly riding up and down the coast, examining passports with unfailing rigour. They added that it had been their intention to go to Edinburgh, but that they had changed their

---

[1] In Scotland, the vassals were invariably of the party to which their chief belonged, whether it was that of the house of Stuart or that of the house of Hanover.

minds due to the impossibility of doing so. They mentioned the names of several of our comrades who had been taken prisoner during the past few days while attempting to pass the nearest ferry, about twenty miles from Cortachie. They insisted that I should abandon my resolve to proceed south, and remain with them in Glen-Prossen for the time being. However anxious I was to reach Edinburgh, I did not wish to throw away my life with blind precipitancy. My situation was then so critical that the slightest false step or error of judgment would be sure to cost me my life, so I accepted their counsel and agreed to remain with them at Samuel's.

Samuel was an honest man, but extremely poor. We remained in his house for seventeen days, eating at the same table as himself and his family, who had no food other than oatmeal and no drink other than the water from the rivulet that ran through the glen. We breakfasted every morning on a piece of oatmeal bread, which we were able to swallow with the aid of draughts of water; for dinner we boiled oatmeal with water, until it acquired a consistency, and ate it with horn-spoons; and in the evening we poured boiling water over this meal in a dish for our supper. I must admit that although the time during which I was confined to this diet passed very slowly, none of us seemed to suffer from it. On the contrary, we were all exceedingly healthy. We might have obtained some variation of this sorry cheer by sending for it to Cortachie, but we were afraid of doing so. Samuel's mode of living was well known, and any change might have led to suspicion that people were concealed in his house, so we refrained from sending for food lest some ill-disposed person should pass on this information to one of the numerous cavalry detachments passing through Cortachie, which could have led to our capture.

Honest Samuel and his family had scarcely any other food

the whole year round, except perhaps during summer when they mixed a little milk with their oatmeal instead of water. Their manner of living placed them beyond the reach of fortune. They had nothing to fear but poor health, and to this they were less exposed as their frugal and simple mode of life did not fill the body with gross humours, as a more luxurious diet might have done. Their needs were few, their labour could always supply them with the means of subsistence, and they enjoyed a degree of health unknown to those who live in ease and abundance. Their desires were confined to the preservation of their existence and their health, without any ambition to change their station in life or to ameliorate their condition. Content with what they possessed, living without care, sleeping without anxiety, and dying without fear, they wanted nothing more.

Besides the poverty of our fare, which was a considerable and difficult adjustment for me, we were frequently alarmed by detachments of English cavalry making an appearance in the neighbourhood. Samuel had a married daughter who lived at the entrance into the glen, and she served as a sentinel to inform us when there were English detachments at Cortachie. This reassured us during the day, for our sentinel was very exact in acquainting us with everything that passed, but when troops arrived at night we were obliged to protect ourselves by escaping to the neighbouring mountains, where we frequently passed nights in the open air, sometimes during dreadful tempests of wind and rain.

One day our sentinel, who was always attentive and alert, came to inform us that various detachments were hovering about our quarters, and that they had captured Sir James Kinloch, his brothers, and several others who had been in his castle. Mr Ker, formerly a colonel in the service of Spain and an *aide-de-camp* of Prince Charles, had likewise been taken about four miles from us, near the little town of Forfar. She added that a party had searched the castle and the environs of Cortachie in hope of finding Lord Ogilvie, who was then not far from us – as his Lordship has since told me – without us knowing it at the time, that the same party had received information of our presence in Glen-Prossen, and that we ran considerable risk of soon being taken prisoner. We immediately held a council and, as there was no longer any safety for us in Glen-Prossen on account of the detachments with which we were continually being surrounded, we unanimously agreed to quit Samuel's at three o'clock the next morning. Our plan was to return to the Highlands and to fix our abode, for the time being, among the rocks. As a result of this decision, we went to bed at eight o'clock in the evening in order to lay in a stock of sleep before our departure, as we had no hope of sleeping under a roof for some time to come.

8. I Dreamed a Dream

Ihave never been in the habit of giving credence to stories of supernatural intervention, which seem to abound in every country and with which men are deceived from their infancy. Such stories are generally the creations of overheated imaginations, of superstitious old women, or of disordered intellects. That night, however, I had so extraordinary and so incomprehensible a dream that if any other person had related it to me, I should have treated him as a visionary. However, it was later verified to the letter, and I owe my life to the circumstance of my having been so struck with it, incredulous as I was, that I could not resist the impression it left on my mind. I dreamed that, having escaped the pursuits of my enemies and being at the end of all my troubles and sufferings, I happened to be in Edinburgh in the company of Lady Jane Douglas, sister of the Earl of Douglas. I was relating to her everything that had occurred to me since the battle of Culloden, detailing all that had taken place in our army since our retreat from Stirling, including the dangers to which I had been personally exposed in endeavouring to escape death on the scaffold.

When I awoke at six o'clock in the morning, this dream had left so strong an impression on my mind that I thought I still heard the soft voice of Lady Jane Douglas in my ears. All my senses were lulled into a state of profound calm, while I felt at the same time a serenity of soul and tranquillity of mind to which I had been a total stranger since the advent of our misfortunes. I remained in my bed, absent and buried in all manner of reflections, my head leaning on my hand and my elbow supported on my pillow, recalling all the circumstances of my dream and regretting very much that it was only a dream, but wishing to have such dreams frequently, to calm the storms and agitations that devoured my soul owing to the uncertainty of my fate. In the certainty of an inevitable punishment, one can at least resolve to face it with courage and resignation, but what situation is crueller than continual oscillation between hope and despair, a thousand times worse than death itself?

I had passed an hour in this attitude, motionless as a statue, when Samuel entered to tell me that my companions had left at three o'clock in the morning, and to tell me where in the mountains I would find them. He added that he had been twice at my bedside to awaken me before their departure but, seeing me fast asleep, could not find it in his heart to disturb me, convinced as he was of my need to rest before the fatigues I must undergo in the mountains. He advised me to rise without delay, as it was time to depart and his daughter, who would think we had all left, might not be as diligent about signalling the arrival of detachments.

I answered in a composed and serious tone: 'Samuel, I'm going to Edinburgh.'

Poor Samuel stared at me with a foolish and astonished air, and exclaimed: 'Excuse me, my good sir, but are you right in the head?'

'Yes,' I replied, 'my head is perfectly sound. I'm going to Edinburgh, and I leave this evening. Go and tell your daughter I'm still here, and that she must continue her usual watch and let me know if any troops arrive in Cortachie during the course of the day.'

Samuel began to tire me with his protestations, so I imposed silence by telling him, once and for all, that I had made up my mind, and that it was pointless to raise the subject again.

No day ever seemed so long to me. My mind was preoccupied with all manner of reflections, agitated in turn by impatience and fear. A thousand gloomy thoughts crowded my mind: the detachments of soldiers; the fanatical zeal of the peasantry (an evil still greater than that of the soldiers); the towns and villages I had to pass through, all filled with Calvinists, bitter enemies of the house of Stuart; and the risks I would have to run applying to boatmen to cross the arm of the sea. The dangers were magnified in my eyes, and I trembled with dread at the very idea of the difficulties to be overcome. However, nothing could shake my resolution to go south to Edinburgh, or perish in the attempt.

I always concluded such reflections by saying to myself, as though in conversation with another: 'Well, then, I must perish! But it's all the same to me whether I'm taken going south or in the Highlands, for there's danger everywhere. If I can only reach Edinburgh, I'll be safer there than in the Highlands, where I have neither friends nor relations, and where all my acquaintances are recent. If I'm taken my fate will soon be decided, and I won't be obliged to languish a long time in the utmost misery as I would if I headed for the mountains, and perhaps that wouldn't save me from the scaffold anyway.' Such were my reflections, and I could think of no better reasons for the decision I had made to proceed south, for it had to be admitted that all the appearances were against me. But my head was so filled with my dream that, even if the whole world had endeavoured to dissuade me from my purpose, it would have made no difference.

Eventually the night, so impatiently awaited, arrived. I mounted my horse with Samuel behind me, as he had consented to act as my guide to the first arm of the sea, some twenty miles from Cortachie. On our way there was a small town called Forfar, one of the most famous for Presbyterian fanaticism, whose inhabitants had lately signalled their holy zeal by contributing to the arrest of Colonel Ker. Samuel informed me that we would have to pass through this infernal town as there was no other road to Broughty, the village on the shore of the first arm of the sea where all roads to the south converge. Later that evening, therefore, we started to pass through this execrable town, its worthless inhabitants deeply buried in sleep. However, no sooner had we entered this abominable place when a dog began to bark, frightening out of his wits poor Samuel, at bottom an honest man, though naturally a coward and poltroon. Seized with panic and terror, he lost control of his senses and endeavoured by every means to throw himself from the horse, and take to his heels. I seized the skirts of his coat and succeeded in keeping him mounted, in spite of his best efforts to disengage himself. I could not afford the risk that his terror, which had deprived him of the use of his reason, would cause him to run away and leave me in the most perplexing dilemma, being wholly unacquainted with this part of the country. I would not even have been able to find my way back to Cortachie without asking at every village, thereby exposing myself to the risk of being taken prisoner by a vile rabble.

Samuel struggled continuously to get down, but I prevented him by the hold I had on his coat. I exhorted him to be quiet, I reproached him, I alternatively entreated and menaced him, but all in vain. He no longer knew what he was about, and it was to no avail that I assured him it was only the barking of a dog. He heard nothing I said and was completely beside himself, perspiring at every pore and trembling like a person *in extremis*.

Fortunately I had an excellent horse. The day after the battle of Culloden, when I was opposite the castle of Macpherson of Clunie and the jade that had saved me from the field of battle was no longer able to stand on its legs, and was ready to sink beneath me, I had met Lady Macpherson in the high road. She told me that seven or eight gentlemen had just abandoned their horses nearby in order to escape on foot into the mountains, so I had taken one of the best of them. Clapping spurs to it, I now galloped through Forfar at full speed, to extricate myself from this troublesome alarm as swiftly as possible. As soon as we were out of the town, and as no one had stirred, Samuel began to breathe again. He recovered his equilibrium, made a thousand apologies for his behaviour, and promised, upon his word, that he would decidedly not allow himself to get into such a plight again, whatever may befall.

When daylight began to appear, I dismounted and offered my horse to Samuel as a present. I was no longer able to keep him as I needed to cross the first arm of the sea, from which we were now about four miles distant. Samuel refused to accept, however, saying that if his neighbours saw him in possession of a fine horse, they would immediately suspect that he had received it from some rebel he had assisted to escape, they would immediately inform against him and he would in consequence be prosecuted. The horse would be the evidence against him, and he would inevitably be sentenced to be hanged. I removed the saddle and bridle, which we threw into a draw-well, and we then drove the horse into a field some distance from the road, so that those who found him might take him for a stray. We had great difficulty in getting rid of this animal, for he followed us for some time like a dog.

We had not walked a quarter of an hour after giving liberty to my horse when we fell in with a friend of Samuel, who questioned him a great deal as to where he was heading, the nature of his business, and who I was. Samuel answered without the least hesitation, which pleasantly surprised me after the adventure of the dog at Forfar: 'I'm going to bring home a calf I left to winter in the Lowlands last autumn. I'm taking this young man with me out of charity, as he was without bread and he serves me for his victuals. I intend sending him back with the calf, whilst I myself go to Dundee to buy a cow with which to support my family during the summer.'

As there happened to be an alehouse nearby, the two friends agreed to have a bottle of beer together, and I was obliged to accompany them. I showed such respect for my newfound master that I did not venture to sit down beside him until he invited me. The friend of Samuel pressed me to partake of their small beer, which tasted for all the world like physic, but Samuel excused me, extolling so much my sobriety and good character that his friend incessantly showed me a thousand little attentions, expressing the wish, from time to time, to find a lad like me on the same terms. I thought I perceived in him a secret desire to entice me from Samuel's service.

After they had swallowed a considerable quantity of beer, they left the alehouse and, to my great pleasure, parted, for not only was I frequently very embarrassed at having to play the part Samuel had assigned me, I was also sick and tired of their mundane jargon. This man had scarcely left us when Samuel whispered in my ear that he was one of the greatest knaves and cheats in this part of the country, famous for his villainy; that if he had found out who I was, he would undoubtedly have betrayed me; and that the mere wish to obtain possession of my watch and purse would have been a sufficient inducement for him to have reported my presence to the authorities and thus sent me to the gallows. I was the more astonished at what Samuel told me as, from their conversation, which was full of assurances of mutual esteem, I had had no doubt in my mind that they entertained for each other the most sincere friendship. Having gained this insight, I greatly praised my new master for his prudence and discretion on this occasion.

Artifice, hypocrisy, and the art of deceiving, which have very improperly been called policy, are commonly supposed to be found only in the courts of princes – the only schools for learning falsehood and dissimulation. But I saw as much finesse and duplicity in the false assurance of friendship and the compliments of these two peasants while they were drinking their beer, and I was as completely duped in this case, as I later was in a conversation at which I happened to be present between two noblemen of the first rank.[1] One of these was my particular friend, and the other an ambassador at a court where he had promised, and where he had had it in his power if he had been so inclined, to be of essential service to my friend, then outlawed and exiled from his native country. These two personages embraced each other with an air of cordiality, said a thousand flattering things to each other, and repeatedly expressed the strongest assurances of mutual friendship, but the moment the ambassador terminated his visit and took his departure, my friend informed me that they cordially detested each other. When I reproached him with having acted a part unworthy of a man of honour and a gentleman, he replied that he had only wished to pay the ambassador in his own coin. Nevertheless, the pantomime of these two lords would have deceived me less, from the opinion generally entertained of the duplicity of courtiers, than that which was acted out by these two peasants.

---

[1] The Duke de Mirepoix, then ambassador at the court of London, and Lord Ogilvie, now Earl of Airly.

9. First Arm of the Sea

At about nine o'clock in the morning, half a league from the ferry but not knowing as yet how I could approach it, to whom I should apply for assistance, or where to find asylum until a favourable opportunity for crossing over should present itself, I asked Samuel if he knew of any gentleman in the neighbourhood of Broughty, not hostile to the house of Stuart, but who had not been in our army. 'That I do,' said Samuel. 'Here is the castle of Mr Graham of Duntroon, who answers precisely to your description. His two nephews were in your army, but he remained quietly at home without declaring himself.'

I did not know Mr Graham, having never seen him, but I had frequently heard my sister speak of him, his niece having been the companion of Lady Rollo, her mother-in-law. Mr Graham was of a very ancient family, one of those who had taken up arms in favour of the house of Stuart in the year 1715. After that unfortunate affair he had entered the service of the English East India Company and attained the command of one of their ships, by which means he had acquired a considerable fortune and raised his family.

I immediately despatched Samuel to inform him that he had brought an unfortunate gentleman, who wished very much to speak to him, to the vicinity of his house. Samuel soon returned and told me that Mr Graham had ordered him to conduct me to one of his enclosures where there was very high broom and where he would soon join me, which he did without delay. I told him who I was and earnestly entreated him to procure me a boat in order to pass the ferry at Broughty as, from his vicinity to it, he must certainly be acquainted with all the inhabitants on whom any reliance could be placed. He replied that it would give him the greatest pleasure to be of use to me, that he knew my sister, whom he had recently seen at the castle of Lord Rollo, and after a thousand apologies for not daring to take me to his castle on account of his servants, of whose fidelity he was not assured, he told me that he would instantly send to Broughty for a boat. He asked me at the same time what I wanted for breakfast. I answered that, after passing seventeen days with Samuel with nothing but oatmeal and water, he could send me nothing that would come amiss and to which my appetite would not do justice. He left and soon after sent his gardener, in whose fidelity he could confide, with new-laid eggs, butter, cheese, a bottle of white wine and another of beer. I never ate with such voracity, and in no time at all devoured seven or eight eggs, with a great quantity of bread, butter and cheese.

Mr Graham returned to the enclosure but, finding me drowsy, soon left me with an assurance that he would immediately send to Broughty to engage boatmen to transport me to the other side of the Firth during the course of the night. Having dismissed Samuel with a gratification beyond his hopes, I lay down among the broom, which was at least four feet high, and slept until one o'clock, when I was agreeably woken by Mr Graham with the good news that he had engaged boatmen to carry me across the Firth at about nine o'clock in the evening.

Mr Graham asked me what I wanted for dinner, naming various good things in his larder, all of which appeared exquisite to one who had undergone such a rigorous Lent at Samuel's. Among other things he mentioned a piece of beef, and I begged him to send me nothing else. Although it was not more than three hours since I had eaten plentifully, my stomach already felt empty and the beef seemed more delicious than anything I had ever tasted before. I felt justified in making an ample repast on this occasion as I was uncertain whether, or when, I would again have such an opportunity. Mr Graham returned immediately after dinner, bringing with him an excellent bottle of old claret which we drank together, after which I felt strong and courageous enough to attempt anything. He then disclosed the arrangements he had made. At precisely five o'clock I was to climb over the wall of the enclosure at a place he pointed out to me, and there I would see the gardener with a sack of corn on his back. I was to follow him at some distance until he entered a windmill. An old woman would then take the place of the gardener, and I was to follow her in the same manner to the village of Broughty. Mr Graham kept me company until four o'clock, when he took his leave after embracing me and wishing me success. I regulated my watch by his, that I might be exact in my appointment with the gardener.

I still had an hour to remain in the enclosure. Due no doubt to my impatience, this seemed extremely long and tedious and I kept my watch constantly in my hand, counting every minute until the hand touched five, when I began to follow Mr Graham's instructions. I had no difficulty spotting the gardener with the sack of corn on his back, but I was very much at a loss to discern the correct old woman among the three or four who happened to pass the windmill at the very moment the gardener entered it, and I did not know, therefore, whom I ought to follow – until mine, seeing my embarrassment, made a sign with her head, which I understood perfectly well. As soon as we arrived at the top of the hill above the village of Broughty, she stopped to tell me that she would go by herself, to see if all was in readiness. She told me to wait for her return in the road where she left me.

Broughty was situated on the sea side, and was not visible until one reached the top of the hill from which the road descended obliquely to the village. The sun was just going down when the good woman left me, and I waited more than half an hour for her in the road. In my impatience I decided to leave the road, and advanced five or six paces into a ploughed field, approaching the brink of the hill. There I lay down in a furrow that gave me a vantage from which I would be able to see her when she began to ascend the hill on her return journey. I had not been in the furrow five minutes, watching for the old woman, when I heard a movement and saw a head, which at first I took to be hers. When I also saw the head of a horse, however, I lay down as before, flat on the ground, with my face towards the road, and saw eight or ten horsemen pass the very place in the road I had left a short while before. The horsemen had scarcely passed when the old woman, who had followed them closely, arrived quite out of breath. I immediately rose and approached her.

'Ah,' said she, in a transport of joy, but trembling nervously, 'I didn't expect to find you here.'

I begged her to calm herself and breath easily, not realising at first what she was referring to. As soon as she had regained her composure sufficiently, she explained the cause of her alarm. The horsemen I had seen pass were English dragoons who had been searching the village with such strictness, and making use of such threats, that they had frightened the boatmen Mr Graham had engaged to carry me over the arm of the sea – to such an extent that they now absolutely refused to perform their engagement. I censured her for her imprudence and thoughtlessness in not advising me that there were dragoons in the village, for not only had I run the risk of being carried off by this detachment, I had several times, in my impatience, been tempted to go down to the village by myself. Had I known the whereabouts of the alehouse in Broughty, or had I thought that I could find it without asking from door to door, I should almost certainly have done so. I would thereby have delivered myself into the mouth of the lion through the folly and stupidity of this woman, who thus nearly allowed me to wander within the shadow of the scaffold.

What exposure to danger is as vulnerable as that in which our lives depend on the discretion of weak people? She told me that on entering the public house to find the boatmen, she was so alarmed on seeing it filled with soldiers that she lost all presence of mind and no longer knew what to do.

At a time when I had begun to think of my escape as almost certain due to an arrangement to be transported across this arm of the sea, the sudden refusal of the boatmen came as a dreadful blow to me. I entreated the old woman to conduct me to the house where the boatmen were, but she had no inclination to return, and excused herself by saying that it was quite useless to do so. The boatmen had been so intimidated by the menaces of the soldiers, she said, that they would not carry me over that night for all the money in the world. She told me that my wisest plan would be to return to Mr Graham, who would find the means of concealing me until the following night, when the boatmen would have recovered from their alarm. I could not abide the idea of turning back, and when I considered that I was now on the shore of that very arm of the sea which had caused me so much uneasiness, that it was the most difficult to pass – on account of its proximity to the mountains and the detachments of dragoons continuously patrolling in its vicinity – and that if I were so disposed I could overcome this difficulty, I became more and more determined to advance. I hoped to persuade the boatmen, either by money or by fair words, and I therefore assured the old woman that I would never have a more favourable opportunity than I did then. The dragoons, having discovered no trace of any rebels, would not think of examining the village a second time the same night. At length she yielded to my entreaties and consented, although with considerable repugnance, to conduct me to the village.

As soon as I entered the public house, the landlady, Mrs Burn, whispered in my ear that I had nothing to fear in her house as her own son had been in our army with Lord Ogilvie. I regarded this as a very good omen. She immediately pointed out to me the boatmen who had promised Mr Graham to transport me to the other side of the Firth. I approached them immediately, but found them trembling with fear as a result of the threats of the soldiers, and all my offers, prayers and solicitations were of no avail. Having spent half an hour vainly trying to persuade them, I noticed – from the glances they bestowed upon them from time to time – that Mrs Burn's two daughters, who were as beautiful as Venus, were not objects of indifference to these boatmen. I therefore quitted the stupid boatmen and attached myself to these two pretty girls, with a view to winning them over to my purpose and thereby availing myself of their influence with the boatmen, as a mistress is naturally all-powerful with her lover. I caressed them, I embraced them, the one after the other, and I said a thousand flattering and agreeable things to them. Indeed, it cost me very little to act this part, for they were exceedingly beautiful and the compliments I paid them were sincere and flowed from the heart. As I had resolved to sleep at Mrs Burn's in case I did not succeed in crossing the Firth, I dismissed the old woman.

In less than half an hour these two beauties had been successfully won over to my purpose, and each of them made a vigorous assault on her sweetheart, using all manner of prayers and entreaties, but with a total lack of success. The fear of these timid animals was more powerful than their love. At length the elder of the two lasses, the beautiful and charming Mally Burn, disgusted and indignant at the obstinacy of the boatmen, said to her sister: 'O, Jenny, they are despicable cowards and poltroons. I would not for the world that this unfortunate gentleman were taken in our house. I pity his situation. Will you take an oar? I'll take the other, and we will row him over ourselves, to the eternal shame of these pitiful and heartless cowards.' Jenny consented without hesitation, and I clasped them in my arms, covering them in turn with a thousand tender kisses.

I thought at first that the generous resolution of these girls would influence their admirers, but the unfeeling cowards were not the least bit moved. They preserved their phlegm and allowed the charming girls to act as they pleased, without being the least bit affected by their conduct. Seeing the obstinacy of the boatmen and wishing to take advantage of the offer of my female friends, I immediately took the two oars on my shoulders and proceeded to the shore, accompanied by these two beauties. I launched the boat, pushed it into deep water as soon as we were all three aboard, and, taking one of the oars myself, gave the second to one of the girls, to be relieved by the other when she found herself fatigued.

I experienced on this occasion the truth of the maxim that every kind of knowledge may be useful. When I had been in Russia, where parties of pleasure on the water were frequent, I had sometimes amused myself with rowing, little knowing that I should one day be obliged to row for my life.

We left Broughty at ten o'clock in the evening and reached the opposite shore of this arm of the sea, about two miles in breadth, towards midnight. The weather was fine, and the night was sufficiently clear from the light of the stars to enable me to distinguish the roads. The two beauties landed with me to guide me to the highway leading to St Andrews, and I then took my leave of them, deeply affected by their generous sentiments and heroic courage. I experienced genuine regret on leaving them, mindful that I would probably never see them again. I embraced each of them a thousand times, and as they would not accept any money, I contrived to slip ten or twelve shillings into the pocket of the charming Mally, one of the most perfect beauties nature ever formed. Under any other circumstances they would have tempted me to prolong my stay in their village, and if fortune had ever permitted me to return to my native country, I should certainly have gone to Broughty for the express purpose of visiting them.

10. Between Two Arms

I was never able, beforehand, to form any fixed plan as to what I should do or what road I should take. A thousand obstacles, difficult to surmount, sprang up at every step, yet at the same time unforeseen circumstances frequently operated in my favour. While on the run I had been unable to think of a single person I knew in the whole area between the two arms of the sea, as most of the gentlemen of Fifeshire had taken up arms in favour of Prince Charles and were in the same situation as me. At length, however, it occurred to me to apply to Mrs Spence, a relative who had an estate in the neighbourhood of St Andrews and generally resided in that town. But St Andrews was always the most fanatical town in all Scotland, famous for the assassination – in former times – of its archbishop, Cardinal Beaton. It was full of that accursed race of Calvinists, hypocrites who cloaked their crimes with the veil of religion, who were fraudulent and dishonest in their dealings, and who carried their holy dissimulation so far as to remove their bonnets to say grace when they took even a pinch of snuff. They had the name of God constantly in their mouths, and hell in their hearts, and no town ever so much deserved the fate of Sodom and Gomorrah. However, I resolved to go there as it was a sea port, the hope of being able to find a passage to a foreign country through the means of Mrs Spence operating as a strong inducement.

I travelled all night and, when daylight began to appear, sat down on the banks of a stream to ease my feet, as my toes were bruised and cut to the bone by my coarse peasant's stockings and shoes. When I removed my shoes I found that my feet were bleeding, but bathing them eased the pain considerably. I kept my feet in the stream for two hours, during which time I felt a sweet serenity pervade my whole being, despite the fact that I was worn out with fatigue and in such a condition as to excite compassion in the hardest heart. I felt ready to die, and invoked the Supreme Being, with great fervour, to take pity on my sufferings and bring my miserable existence to a swift end. The prospect of death, however alarming it may have been at other times, was then nothing terrible to me. On the contrary, I viewed my dissolution as the greatest good that could befall me. I bitterly regretted that I had not met my fate in the battle of Culloden, where I had escaped so narrowly, and envied the fate of my comrades who had died on the field of battle. The horrendous idea of the hangman with a knife in his hand, ready to open my body whilst yet alive, to tear out my heart, and to throw it into the fire, still palpitating – the punishment inflicted on all those who had the misfortune to be taken and condemned – haunted my imagination. I could not banish the fear that I too would be taken, and the prospect of perishing on a scaffold in this manner, in presence of a brutal and cruel populace, almost tempted me to abridge my days on the banks of this stream. My life had become a burden, and under such circumstances existence itself seemed meaningless. Fortunately, however, the wretched are never slow to embrace the illusion of hope. They see nothing in their projects but the termination of their misfortunes, and all their calculations are founded on that hope. I beseeched the Almighty that, if it was my fate to perish by the executioner, he would at least prevent me from languishing any longer between life and death, in this cruel state of uncertainty.

I put on my stockings and shoes, and rose to proceed on my way, but found that I could scarcely stand upright. My stockings and shoes were hardened with blood, and I felt a pain that cut me to the heart as soon as I attempted to stir. So I removed them again, and put my feet once more in the water. Having soaked my stockings and shoes in the stream for half an hour to soften them, I found myself able to walk, and proceeded on my journey. After an hour I met a countryman who told me I was still four miles from St Andrews. I flattered myself that he was mistaken, but discovered in due course that these four miles were as long as the leagues in the environs of Paris. I arrived at St Andrews at about eight o'clock in the morning, very much fatigued. It was Sunday, and the streets were filled with people who continually stopped me to learn any news of the rebels. I answered that I knew nothing of them as I had only come from Dundee, a town almost as fanatical as St Andrews itself. I enquired after Mrs Spence's house on entering the town and, having found it, told her maid-servant that I had a letter for her mistress which I must deliver into her own hands. She conducted me to Mrs Spence's chambers, where she was still in bed, and immediately retired. My cousin did not at first recognise me under my disguise but, after examining me for a while, she exclaimed, shedding a flood of tears: 'Ah, my dear child, you are inevitably lost. How could you think of coming to St Andrews, and especially to a house so much suspected as mine?'

'The mob yesterday,' added she, 'arrested the son of my neighbour, Mr Ross, who was disguised like you as a countryman, before he had been a quarter of an hour in his father's house. He is now loaded with irons in the prison of Dundee.'

I did not expect such a reception, but, sensible of the false step I had taken, I was very anxious to extricate myself from it. I therefore entreated her to calm herself, as contrary conduct would be the surest means of ruining me by exciting suspicion in her servants. As soon as she had recovered herself a little, therefore, she wrote a letter to her farmer, who lived a quarter of a league from the town, requesting him to give me a horse and to conduct me to Wemyss. This village was on the shore of the arm of the sea I had yet to cross before reaching Edinburgh, about ten miles distant from St Andrews. This was exactly what I most desired, for I was overcome with fatigue and with the deplorable state of my feet. She stated in the letter to her farmer that she was sending me to Edinburgh with papers that were urgently wanted, nay, absolutely necessary, for a lawsuit that was to be decided in that city in the course of a few days. I immediately took leave of my cousin, without sitting down in her house, and set off with a little girl she sent to conduct me to her farmer, taking byroads through gardens to avoid appearing in the streets of this execrable town. As soon as I was fairly out of the town, the welcome prospect of obtaining a horse to Wemyss gave me renewed courage and vigour to endure my sufferings.

I delivered my letter to the farmer, and the answer I received from this brute petrified me. 'Mrs Spence,' he said, 'may take her farm from me and give it to whomsoever she pleases, but she cannot make me profane the Lord's day by giving my horse to one who means to travel upon the Sabbath.' I represented to him, with all the energy of which I was capable, the necessity of having his horse on account of Mrs Spence's lawsuit, and the great loss which any delay in transmitting her papers to her advocate might occasion, but all my urgings had no effect on him and he obstinately persisted in his refusal.

This holy rabble never scrupled to deceive and cheat their neighbours on the Lord's day, as well as on other days, nor to shed the blood of such unfortunate gentlemen as they made prisoners in their infernal excursions, although they had done them no harm and were even unknown to them. These hypocrites, the execration and refuse of the human race, with their eyes continually turned towards heaven, availed themselves of everything that was sacred as a mask with which to deceive, and unfortunately this spirit of hypocrisy is to be found equally in all religions.

Frustrated in my hopes of obtaining a horse, I immediately quitted the house of the farmer and took the road to Wemyss. What a dreadful situation! The wounds in my feet were so painful I could hardly breathe. Not knowing anyone to turn to in the village of Wemyss, if I should be able to walk the ten miles, and mindful of the risk I should run of being seized in any public house where I might spend the night – in short, not knowing what to do or what to make of myself – I fortunately came to a stream half a league from the infernal town. I went about a musket-shot from the road and, having removed my shoes and stockings, I found the wounds in my feet considerably augmented, with blood flowing from them in torrents. I bathed my feet as before, and soaked my shoes and stockings, which were full of blood, but lameness was not my greatest misfortune. My mind was as much lacerated and tormented as my body. The hopes I had fondly cherished, of receiving asylum and assistance from my cousin Spence, had vanished into thin air, and the twelve long miles from Broughty to St Andrews had been travelled in vain.

I tortured my imagination to think of some resource, but came up with nothing. The castle of Lord Rollo was on the same side of the arm of the sea, but it was twenty-five miles west of St Andrews. I was convinced of the friendship of his lordship and of the good wishes of the whole family, but how was it possible, exhausted with fatigue and lame as I then was, to get there? It would be a journey of several days for me. Besides, supposing I should be able to reach it, it was still further from Edinburgh than the place where I then was. I knew not what to do. However, as I could think of no other feasible alternative, I decided at length to follow that course and go there by short journeys, sleeping always in the fields and avoiding as much as possible the towns and villages that lay in my way.

With my body worn out from pain and fatigue, and although my mind was cruelly agitated and lost in a labyrinth of reflection, I suddenly remembered a chambermaid of my mother, married two years before to George Lillie, gardener to Mr Beaton of Balfour, whose mansion was about half a league from the village of Wemyss. As this woman had taken great care of my mother during a long illness, my father, as a reward for her attachment, had paid for her wedding. I knew that Lillie was a Calvinist, and the most furious and extravagant fanatic in that part of the country, but in consequence of the kindness shown to him by my family, I was not afraid of any treachery on his part, even if he should refuse to render me any service. If he received me into his house, I knew I would be secure with him. The recollection of Lillie and his wife produced such an instantaneous effect on me that I immediately jumped up to walk, without thinking of my stockings and shoes, and without perceiving that I had not sufficiently reposed myself. Although it was no more than a quarter of an hour since I had sat down, I no longer felt uneasiness or pain.

I had eaten nothing since my repast in the enclosure at Duntroon, and though Mr Graham had made me fill my pockets with bread and cheese, my mind had been too troubled to allow me to feel hunger. My appetite returned, however, with my hope of finding refuge with Lillie. Drawing the bread and cheese from my pocket, I made a hearty meal of it while my shoes and stockings were still soaking in the water. My strength and courage returned at the same time and, after resting for a couple of hours, I put paper over the wounds on my feet to prevent the friction of my coarse stockings and shoes, and proceeded on my journey, walking six miles without halting.

I had now travelled halfway from St Andrews to Wemyss, and had only to walk four miles to reach Balfour. My impatience to get there made me feel the fatigue and pain less acutely. On the way I found another stream, where I rested and bathed my feet once more. My toes were now in the most wretched condition, bruised and cut to the bone, and the marks of these wounds will remain with me for as long as I live. Indeed, the second toe of my left foot was battered quite out of joint on this cruel day. However, my sufferings, poignant as they were, did not prevent me from finishing the remaining four miles to Balfour, and I arrived there at about nine o'clock in the evening, with a joy and satisfaction surpassing all imagination.

When I found myself within a pace of Lillie's house, I eagerly seized the door handle with both hands, to prevent myself from falling to the ground. My strength was totally depleted and I felt unable to take another step, not even to escape the scaffold. It is amazing to consider the additional strength we derive from necessity, from the desire to preserve our existence, and the incredible efforts we are able to make under such circumstances. When I knocked, Lillie opened the door, but did not recognise me in my disguise as a beggar. He said several times, with impatience and evident alarm: 'Who are you? What is your business? Whom do you want?'

I made no reply, but advanced through the door lest he should shut it in my face. This added to his alarm, and it was evident that he took me for a robber or housebreaker, for he trembled from head to foot. I asked him if there were any strangers in the house. His wife, who was sewing near the fire, knew my voice and, perceiving my dress, called out to her husband: 'Good God, I know him. Quick, shut the door!'

Lillie obeyed without examining me further and, following me to the light, recognised me himself. I could scarcely suppress a laugh, notwithstanding my pain, at his look of amazement. Confounded, lost in astonishment, petrified, he clasped his hands and exclaimed with uplifted eyes: 'O, this does not surprise me! My wife and I were talking about you last night, and I said I would bet anything in the world that you were with that accursed race.'

I answered that he was right to conclude that I had been, from the principles of attachment to the house of Stuart in which I had been raised. 'But, at present, my good George,' I continued, 'you must aid me in escaping the gallows.'

It was a severe and humiliating trial for Lillie to be obliged, from considerations of gratitude, to give asylum to a rebel, and to find himself needing to succour one of the very men he had so loudly condemned. No one in that neighbourhood had, on public occasions, held forth with more zeal and eloquence against the Pope and the Pretender, who were always coupled together. He was, however, an honest man, notwithstanding his fanatical principles, and he assured me that he was deeply affected by my situation and would do everything in his power to save me and to procure me a crossing to the other side as soon as possible. Finding that I was utterly helpless and incapable of stirring either arm or leg, Lillie and his wife removed my shoes and stockings, and as all gardeners in Scotland had an empirical knowledge of medicine, Lillie first bathed my feet with whisky, which made me suffer the most excruciating pain, and then applied a salve to them. They then drew on a pair of Lillie's stockings and slippers, after which I found myself relieved and quite a new man.

I sent Lillie with my compliments to Mr Beaton, his master, begging him not to take it amiss if his gardener should not be at his work at the usual hour, as I was concealed in his house and in need of his services. Mr Beaton immediately sent Lillie back to tell me that he was exceedingly sorry that he could not wait on me in person as he had been unwell for some time past, and was just then going to bed; that he was also unable to offer me a bed in his house, where I would have been more conveniently lodged than at Lillie's; but that he begged me most earnestly to send freely to him for whatever I might need. He had wanted Lillie to take with him some wine, fowls and other articles, but whatever desire Lillie might have had that I should fare well in his house, he very prudently refused this offer lest, as he told me, it should have aroused suspicion amongst Mr Beaton's servants that he had someone concealed in his house. I praised Lillie highly for his prudence and discretion.

Mrs Lillie prepared for my supper a dish of steaks, which I devoured in haste as I had more inclination to sleep than to eat, having been two days and two nights on my feet without any sleep except during the few hours I had passed in the enclosure of Mr Graham. Lillie undressed me and carried me to bed in his arms as it was impossible for me to put a foot to the ground. I slept without waking from ten o'clock that evening until half-past nine the following evening. Mrs Lillie took particular care not to make the slightest noise, nor would she even wake me to receive a visit from Mr Beaton.

As nothing restores an exhausted frame so much as sleep, I found myself greatly refreshed and in all respects well, except that I still suffered greatly from my feet. Mrs Lillie had a fowl ready to put to the fire as soon as I awoke, and I ate it in bed. Lillie removed the dressing he had applied to my feet, and replaced it with another. He told me that his mother-in-law kept a public house in the village of Wemyss, much frequented by fishermen, and that she might be able to procure some person of her acquaintance to carry me across the arm of the sea. He proposed that I should accompany him to her house if I were in a condition to walk. I was not sorry that, in his desire to get rid of me, Lillie was as eager for me to escape as I was myself. He offered me a horse at the instance of Mr Beaton but, before accepting it, I wished to try my strength to see whether I could undertake the journey on foot. Having risen, I walked around the room supported on Lillie's arm, and found that I could do without the horse. While I had slept Mrs Lillie had been good enough to cut off the feet of my coarse stockings, and to sew stuff soles onto them, but I still suffered a great deal from my feet.

We set out at about half-past ten that night. Suspended rather than resting on the arm of Lillie, I walked with difficulty, but the hope of finding an opportunity to cross this arm of the sea and of reaching Edinburgh made me endure a pain that, at any other time, would have been unendurable. While we were on the road, I said to him jocularly: 'My good Lillie, if I should actually be taken in your company, what a figure you would cut. You would never dare show your face again in any of your holy assemblies. Your reputation as a good Calvinist would be ruined forever.'

He heaved a deep sigh, and replied: 'Ah, sir, do not speak of that.'

I burst out laughing, and continued: 'It may be true, Lillie, that you wouldn't be disembowelled alive like me, but your character with your brethren would be lost forever.'

I amused myself on the road with similar observations, and took some pleasure in remarking that he considered his honour to be fully engaged, and would try every means to procure me a passage, as much from the fear of being discovered in my company as from the desire to curry favour with my family and appear meritorious in their eyes.

When we arrived at the house of his mother-in-law, she told us that of all the fishermen of Wemyss, she knew no one on whom we could rely except a person by the name of Salmon. She added that he was an ardent Calvinist and a violent enemy of the house of Stuart, but that in other respects he was an honest man and much distinguished in the village for his probity and good conduct. She thought we might apply to him with perfect safety as, in case he was not disposed to assist us, he was too honest a man to do us any injury.

We immediately went to Salmon's. It was close to midnight, and we found him already up and preparing his nets to go out fishing. As he knew Lillie's voice, he opened the door to us. Lillie, after considerable struggles with himself, at length broke his silence and, in a plaintive tone of voice and with an air of humility, shame and embarrassment, said: 'My friend Salmon, this is the only son of the mistress of my wife. He has been imprudent and foolish enough to join that accursed race which seeks to destroy our religion and enslave us. You see, my friend, the dreadful predicament in which he has landed himself. Everyone knows the kindness his family showed to my wife and me at our marriage. I honour and respect them, and I am much afraid that, if he were taken, it would be the death of both his mother and his father, for they are greatly attached to him. I come, my friend Salmon, to entreat you, with uplifted hands, to give him a passage tomorrow in your boat, when you go to Leith to sell your fish.'

The pathetic manner in which Lillie spoke to Salmon gave me great pleasure, but the answer, pronounced in a rough voice, pleased me not at all, and left me little hope of success. 'You deserve, indeed,' said Salmon, 'to have your life saved, you who wished to abolish our holy religion, destroy our liberties, and make slaves of us all. No, Lillie, he applies to the wrong person when he comes to me. I will do him no harm. I am not capable of informing against him. He is in perfect safety in that respect, but he must not expect me to do him any service. I will not assist any of that accursed race of rebels.'

I offered him all the money I still possessed, about six

guineas, to convey me over the next morning in his boat, but he would hear no more on the subject. Although he was not to be won over by money, as he was adamant and bore the stamp of an honest man on his countenance – a much more expressive mirror than his gesture, his language, or even his accent – I could not think of abandoning my enterprise. I had offered him all my money without the slightest effect, but I still hoped to win him over through his feelings. As he kept an alehouse, I asked him to at least do me the honour of drinking a bottle of beer with us. He consented, and I did not spare the beer, taking glass for glass with them – without, however, speaking a single word about my passage, but always attentive to insinuate myself into his good graces in order to render him favourable to my purpose.

After passing an hour in this way, he turned to Lillie and said: 'What a pity this poor young man should have been so debauched and perverted by this worthless rebel crew. He's a fine lad.'

Lillie artfully took advantage of this favourable inclination to drop a word or two in my favour, observing that, by that time, I had heartily repented of what I had done. I pretended not to hear them but, seeing that my affairs were moving in an excellent train, I ensured a continued supply of small beer, which by the way was as weak as water. At length I had played my part so well, and gained the friendship of Salmon so completely, that this honest man suddenly offered me a passage in his boat the next morning, and would not hear of any money, being actuated merely by a pure and noble feeling of generosity. Indeed, the part I had to play with poor Salmon was not a difficult one, for he truly was a virtuous man, highly respected by the whole village for his integrity and upright conduct, just as the mother of Mrs Lillie had represented him to me.

A virtuous man is never hard-hearted, but always possesses compassion and humanity for the unfortunate. Virtue always pleases us, in whatever class of men we find it, and we are involuntarily predisposed in favour of the possessor. Hence we do no violence to our own conscience when we say flattering and obliging things to a worthy man, however low his situation in life, unlike when we are obliged to say them to a worthless nobleman of the first rank whose elevation is the product of mere happenstance.

11. Second Arm of the Sea

Salmon co-owned his boat with several other fishermen, and it was therefore necessary for him to manage matters with his associates. He advised me to conceal myself in a cavern, which looked towards the sea, about the distance of a gunshot from Wemyss, until daybreak. It was agreed that as soon as the fishing boats returned to the harbour, I should come down to the boat with Salmon in it and ask if they would carry me across to Leith for money. He would answer in the affirmative, and then settle with his associates as to the price. If anyone in the boat should object, he would endeavour to overcome them. At the same time, Salmon and Lillie taught me the peculiarities of the dialect of that part of the country, which I should adopt for the occasion. When I quitted Salmon, I slipped a guinea into his hand, telling him that it was only earnest money, and he clearly had difficulty accepting it, observing that I ought to know that it was not pecuniary interest that motivated him to render me this service. Lillie, having accompanied me to the cavern, took his leave to return home, offering me asylum in his house in case this opportunity should fail. Although I now looked upon my passage as certain, I was by no means displeased at the idea of a safe retreat at Lillie's, as it was impossible to foresee what unfortunate incidents might occur.

The cavern was one of the most remarkable antiquities of Scotland. According to tradition, it had in former times been a heathen temple. It had been dug in under a hill, with an entrance about five feet high and three feet wide, the start of the hill being about thirty paces from the seashore. It was very high and spacious within, and appeared to be of immense depth. An adventure, which had happened in this cavern to King James the Fourth of Scotland, had given celebrity to it.

The King, who used to amuse himself by wandering about the country in different disguises, had been overtaken by a violent storm on a dark night, and was obliged to take shelter in the cavern. Having advanced some way in, he discovered a number of men and women ready to begin a roasted sheep by way of supper. From their appearance he began to suspect that he had not fallen in with the best of company, but as it was too late to retreat, he requested their hospitality until the tempest was over. They acquiesced and invited the King, whom they did not recognise, to sit down and partake with them. As soon as they had finished their supper, one of them presented to him a plate on which two daggers were laid in form of a St Andrew's cross, telling the King, at the same time, that this was the dessert they always served to strangers, and that he must choose one of the daggers and fight whomsoever the company should select to attack him. The King retained his presence of mind, instantly seized both daggers – one in each hand – and plunged them into the hearts of the two robbers who were next to him. Running at full speed to the mouth of the cavern, he escaped pursuit in the obscurity of the night, and the next morning he ordered the whole of this band of cutthroats to be seized. They were all hanged.

I went a little way into the cavern and, having thrown myself down on the ground, dozed for about an hour until I was woken by the most terrible and alarming cries I had ever heard. I began at first to suspect the fidelity of Salmon, notwithstanding the highly favourable opinion I had formed of him, imagining that this was a detachment of soldiers sent to take me prisoner. I buried myself in the interior of the cavern, holding a pistol ready-cocked in each hand and advancing always until I could place my back against the wall, in order the better to be able to defend myself. I then began to examine the noise with attention, and from the velocity in the movement of the objects causing the noise, I soon became convinced that it was not caused by men, and it was only men that I dreaded at that time. Sometimes the objects were about my ears and almost stunned me. Then, in an instant, they were at a considerable distance, moving with incredible swiftness and rapidity. At length I terminated my preoccupation with this terrifying and incomprehensible phenomenon, which made a noise and confusion like that of a number of trumpets and drums, with a mixture of different sounds altogether alien to me.

I approached the entrance to the cavern without any further inclination to sleep, and, when daylight began to appear, I fixed my eyes on the sea to observe the movements of the fishing boats, about a quarter of a league from the shore. As soon as I saw them enter the harbour, I left the cavern and followed Salmon's instructions. Unfortunately for me, his boat had been spectacularly unsuccessful, and his associates had obliged him to sell their fish to another boat because, having caught so few fish themselves, it was not worth their while to go to Leith to sell them. I asked if they would give me a passage to Leith for money. Salmon replied: 'Very willingly,' and joined his companions to settle a price with them. They all agreed to take me over for half-a-crown, upon which I felt an inexpressible pleasure.

Having concluded our agreement, I was proceeding to enter the boat when, at that exact moment, Salmon's wife arrived, swearing and bawling that she would not allow her husband to go that day to Leith where he had nothing to do, especially with a stranger. There appeared to her something mysterious about the business, which she could not comprehend. What a terrible disappointment! I cursed this mischievous vixen in my heart, but that availed me nothing; and Salmon, who was the weaker party, was obliged to submit to his wife. I was prudent enough to take no part in their dispute, fearing from the suspicion she showed that she might have overheard our conversation the previous night while we were drinking beer, for I had not been aware that Salmon was married or that his wife was sleeping in the same room we had been in.

I therefore yielded with good grace and with an air of indifference. Salmon proposed that we drink a bottle of beer together, I consented, and as we mounted the stairs he slipped the guinea I had given him into my hand, saying: 'You see, sir, I am not the master. I hope, with all my heart, that you may have the good fortune to escape, and I'm extremely sorry that I have not the means of contributing to it.'

I admired the honesty of Salmon, for not only could he have kept the guinea, he could have informed against me, and thereby gained my purse and my watch as well as the considerable reward paid by the government for every rebel taken prisoner. His generous conduct was the more meritorious because he was a decided enemy of the house of Stuart and totally unacquainted with me. Humanity alone, and a noble soul, had made him act towards me with an elevation of sentiment superior to his condition in life.

I did not wish to proceed directly to the house of Mrs Lillie's mother for, as the accursed fish-woman had announced her suspicions before all and sundry, I was afraid of being followed. I therefore proceeded along the seashore to return to the cavern and, when I came opposite the mouth, I looked about me in every direction before, on seeing no one, quickly darting into it. I felt a strong desire to discover the cause of the extraordinary noise that had disturbed me so much the previous night, and of which I could form no idea. I advanced about thirty or forty paces in the dark, having lost sight of the entrance, when the same loud noise renewed itself. On clapping my hands and shouting, the noise increased a thousand-fold and absolutely stunned me. I even felt the wind caused by the rapid movement of these unknown objects that incessantly approached quite close to me, as if with intent to attack. I drew back until I could see the light from the entrance of the cavern, began to clap my hands again and redouble my shouts, and then I saw numberless owls and other birds fly out. The terrible noise of these birds could not be compared to any sound I had ever heard. Their screams, and the noise of their wings while flying, were confounded together by the echo of the cavern, and composed together a noise that pierced my very ears, while the impetuosity of their flight resembled a tempest. If I had not coolly and thoroughly examined the cause of so singular an effect, I should never have known what to think of it, and might have attributed the adventure to some supernatural agency or given as romantic an account of miracles and ghosts as those related by the good Saint Anthony.

After remaining half an hour in the cavern, I returned to the house of Mrs Lillie's mother-in-law and told her how I had lost the most favourable opportunity for making a crossing of this arm of the sea through the wickedness of Salmon's wife after I had made the proper arrangements with her husband. I earnestly entreated her to endeavour to procure some other person to carry me over as soon as possible, at any price. She immediately ushered a person into my room without having given me any information about him, merely announcing him as an officer of the customs in the service of King George. I imagined that she had either lost her senses or wished to betray me, and I was still more astonished when she began telling him that I had been with Prince Charles. The officer, perceiving my uneasiness, begged me not to be alarmed, adding that he had been in a similar situation in the year 1715; and that, having lost his property, he was reduced to the cruel necessity of accepting a mean employment under the Usurper in order to procure a livelihood, but that his attachment and his hopes for the prosperity of the house of Stuart were unchanged.

Having recovered from my alarm, I enquired whether he could recommend an honest man who would undertake to convey me across the Firth. He replied that there was one, David Cousselain, sexton of the meeting of non-jurors in the village of Wemyss, a very honest man zealously disposed to render any service to all who belonged to the party of Prince Charles. He added that I could not apply to a better man. He immediately went out in quest of him, and they both entered the house after a few minutes.

Cousselain said that he would very willingly take one oar if he could find someone to take the other, and he proposed conducting me to the house of a Mr Robertson in the village of Dubbieside, half a league from Wemyss, in order to borrow his boat. He informed me that Mr Robertson was secretly attached to the Prince's party and would do everything in his power to oblige me. We set off immediately for Dubbieside.

As we had two bad villages to pass through on our way, Cousselain cautioned me, in case any questions were put to me, to call myself John Cousselain, weaver of Culross, the name and trade of his brother whom nobody in that neighbourhood knew. If anyone should suspect me of being a rebel, he would claim me and maintain against all and sundry that I was his brother. I was dreadfully afraid of my new trade as a weaver. When I was merely a servant, it had been easy for me to act my part, as I had done in the services of Mrs Menzie and Samuel, but if I were arrested on suspicion and became obliged to show that I could work at my new trade as a weaver, I knew that the deception would immediately be revealed. There was, however, no trade better suited to me on this occasion.

Mr Robertson told me, with a smile, that he would not lend me his boat, but that he would willingly permit Cousselain to carry it off if he could find another person to assist him in rowing me to the other side. As to himself, he did not know a single person in Dubbieside in whom he felt he could confide, but he advised me to call on a Mr Seton, a gentleman living in Dubbieside, whose eldest son had been in our army. I did not know the father, but I had been an intimate friend of his son, without however being aware that his father lived in Dubbieside. I was delighted to make this discovery.

Having found Mr Seton at home, I acquainted him with my name and my friendship with his son. He immediately asked me to accompany him into the parlour and, once there, he subjected me to an exhausting cross-examination, the significance of which escaped me. He received me in the coldest possible manner, interspersing his questions with abrupt and disjointed observations that left me entirely nonplussed. After harassing me in this manner for half an hour, his son suddenly entered the parlour and clasped me in his arms. He, the son, told me that they had suspected me of being a spy, sent to take him prisoner, and that, although he had examined me from head to foot for half an hour through a hole in the partition of the room, it was only at that moment that he had been able to recognise me beneath my disguise.

I was very glad to see young Seton again, particularly as I had known nothing of his fate since the battle of Culloden, and the pleasure of our reunion was reciprocal. There is always a friendship between persons who have shared the same misfortunes, and he invited me to remain with him at his father's house. This offer was the more agreeable because Dubbieside was conveniently situated for an opportunistic crossing of the nearby arm of the sea.

After a stay of eight days with my friend, at the end of

which I was not one whit nearer my object than on the first day of my arrival, we experienced a great alarm which interrupted the happiness I had begun to enjoy in the amiable society of the Seton family. Miss Seton having asked a fish-woman, while she was cheapening her fish at the door, if there were any news, the fish-woman answered that the general talk was of a rebel seen hovering every day along the coast, as far as Wemyss, who had offered a great deal of money to the fishermen for a passage. She added that he would certainly be caught some day in his excursions. The alarm occasioned by this piece of news can readily be appreciated, especially since I might have been followed as far as Mr Seton's house without realising it. As there was every reason to fear that the house might be searched immediately, my companion in misfortune resolved to quit his father's house the same evening in order to take refuge in the house of a friend, and I decided to return to Lillie's.

Before I left Dubbieside, however, I was determined to make a last effort to cross the arm of the sea that very night. I sent for Cousselain, who came immediately but informed me that, notwithstanding his utmost endeavours, he had been unable to find a single person who would join him in our enterprise. What a deplorable situation, to be so near Edinburgh, where all my wishes centred, yet at the same time feel obliged to retreat, further away from Edinburgh, burying myself in the heart of the country and abandoning all thought of crossing this arm of the sea. The idea of withdrawing instead of advancing threw my mind into the cruellest agitation, and chagrined me beyond measure.

Another Seton, the younger brother of my friend, a youth of eighteen who had made some voyages, seeing my distress and touched by my predicament, generously offered to take an oar with Cousselain to row me across the Firth.

From Dubbieside to Leith, this was about three leagues in breadth. I accepted his obliging offer with both gratitude and determination to avail myself of it, and the attitude I displayed was devoid of anything resembling ceremony. The whole family encouraged him in his good and generous resolution, and we agreed to set out at about nine o'clock that evening. All of a sudden everything seemed to favour me, the passage of this arm of the sea, which had caused me so much trouble and anxiety, now appearing beyond the reach of accident.

But fortune took pleasure in intervening and presenting new obstacles to my deliverance. The noise Seton and Cousselain made when launching the boat alarmed the inhabitants of the village, who were not yet then abed. The cry that a rebel was attempting to escape was immediately heard in every direction, and Seton and Cousselain considered themselves fortunate in being able to escape this hubbub without discovery. I was furious on learning of this cruel twist of fate. I dared not say anything to Seton, for it was kindness alone that had prompted him to assist me, but my rage broke out against Cousselain with double fury. I bitterly reproached him for his stupidity in making so much noise while launching the boat, and treated him with undisguised disdain. Notwithstanding this unfortunate beginning, however, I remained resolved to force the attempt.

Being present myself at the operations, and fortunately – as it turned out – experiencing a rising sense of obstinacy, the more objections were raised against repeating the attempt that night, the more determined I became to press on with it. Mr Seton and his whole family pleaded with me to defer the attempt until the following night, steadfastly maintaining that the inhabitants, being alarmed, would be on the lookout all night, and that it was therefore impossible for me to succeed. I answered that it was useless to speak to me further on the subject, that I was determined to proceed, and that, rather than delay another night, I would if necessary embark alone, with an oar in each hand, and commit myself to Providence. Indeed I most certainly would have done just that, however extravagant the attempt might have appeared, so bent was I on parting, so enraged was I at being unable to find a single honest man among the fishermen who would join Cousselain to save my life, so convinced was I that I had no better prospect for the foreseeable future.

An immovable firmness in my resolutions has always been very useful to me. I have always endeavoured to reflect well before coming to any decision as to what steps I should take, examining with impartiality the reasons for and against any measure, and considering the results that might naturally be expected from it. But having once decided, no person could ever succeed in making me waver in my determination, even in cases where the only alternatives were success or death, and when everyone was against my opinion. I have always found advantage in acting in this manner. Though obstinacy may, generally speaking, be a defect in a man's character, we must know our own affairs better than anyone else and, being the person chiefly interested, our mind exerts itself more to discover the resources we require. Hence, if we are endowed with good sense and judgment, our affairs will always be more successful when we act on our own initiative rather than by reliance on the counsel of others who, frequently, by their doubts, only shake our confidence in our own opinions, and lead us astray.

I told Cousselain to hold himself in readiness at ten o'clock as I wished to make one more attempt, and I gave him money to purchase some refreshment before the passage. He returned at the agreed hour, but so drunk that he could hardly stand, having employed the intervening hour to good effect.

Everything seemed to conspire against me. I cursed and swore, but was determined to persevere. To the new solicitations made to induce me to remain, I replied that Cousselain was only required on the return voyage, that he could sleep and sober up during the passage across while I rowed with Mr Seton, that this was the only inconvenience, and that I would most certainly make my departure that night. I carried Cousselain on my back and stretched him out at the bottom of the boat, which Mr Seton and I launched noiselessly, and, each of us taking an oar, we began to row with all our strength. As soon as we were about fifty paces from the shore, safe from any disturbance from the inhabitants, I began to breathe more easily, and my heart felt relieved of a heavy burden.

A rising easterly wind tossed our little boat dreadfully, and Seton was greatly alarmed. He had good reason to be anxious for, had a wave broken against us, it would have filled our boat with water and sunk it. I kept encouraging him, even though in any other situation I would have been as much alarmed as he was, for with every wave we were in the greatest danger of being swallowed up. But I was then afraid only of the scaffold, and every other danger made only the slightest impression on me. We had another potential danger to deal with in addition to that of the wind and the waves, in the form of a drunk man at the bottom of the boat. Cousselain tried constantly to rise, several times nearly capsising us, so that we were obliged to kick him mercilessly in order to keep him quiet, threatening at the same time to throw him overboard if he made the slightest movement. We had no other means of making him see reason. Seton and I rowed like galley slaves and succeeded in landing, at about six o'clock the next morning, a league and a half to the east of Edinburgh. As the Firth gradually widened in breadth towards the east, we had crossed at least four or five leagues by the time we landed.

I tenderly embraced young Seton, thanking him from the bottom of my soul for the essential services he had rendered me, and I gave Cousselain, who had begun to sober up, a gratification much beyond his hopes. They immediately re-embarked to return to Dubbieside, while I hastened as best I could from the seashore in case some countryman had seen us land.

12. Landed Reflections

No felicity could surpass that which I felt on landing, having surmounted the greatest obstacles to my escape. I was now within reach of the assistance of my relations and friends in Edinburgh. It had not however been without a good deal of pain and difficulty that I had succeeded in crossing, for my hands were now in nearly as bad a plight as my feet had been ten days before, bleeding a great deal and considerably swollen. But I did not much mind being lame in my hands for a few days, as I would not have much occasion to use them, and my feet were now pretty well recovered. Having landed about a musket-shot from Prestonpans, where we had obtained so brilliant a victory over the English, and not daring to approach Edinburgh before dark, I decided to spend the whole day on the field of battle tranquillising my mind a little, softening somewhat the rigours of my fate by reflection on the past.

That place represented a striking symbol of the vicissitudes of fortune to which we humans are subject. I compared my present state with my situation on that glorious day when I had discharged the function of *aide-de-camp* to the Prince, carrying his orders everywhere and charged with the care of thirteen hundred English prisoners. Now I was covered in rags to escape the scaffold, borne down with trouble and distress, and found my only consolation in the hope of escape to a foreign country, with the concomitant abandonment forever of the land of my birth, my relations and my friends. How stark was the contrast. I could not help thinking that Providence had so disposed matters that we should land near the fields of Prestonpans – having been carried so far east by the ebbing of the tide – rather than in the neighbourhood of Leith, where we had intended to land, in order to impress indelibly on my mind the lessons that will never be effaced from it. How I would have enjoyed seeing some of the Prince's favourites, whom the importance formerly conferred on them by their favoured position had rendered insolent, proud and impertinent. I imagined seeing them now, mean, servile and cringing in our altered circumstances. I have indeed seen them since, and I found that I was not wrong in my conjectures. Their behaviour was precisely what I had anticipated.

The instability of fortune ought to teach men the importance of preserving consistency of character. If we do not allow ourselves to be blown up with prosperity, but conduct ourselves always with modesty and humility, we shall not be cast down or become cringing in adversity. Arrogance and vanity are the infallible marks of smallness of soul, and never fail to degenerate, in reverses of fortune, into the meanest servility. A man who is modest, mild and beneficent will never allow himself to descend so low. Whatever revolutions of fortune he may experience, and however exalted the elevation from which he may fall, his misfortune will always be accompanied by the esteem and regret of all good men, and he will always have the public voice in his favour. When happy, everyone will rejoice in his good fortune, and when he experiences reverses, everyone will be eager to console him.

In going over the ground, ever step brought to remembrance some particular of the battle. When I reached the spot where I had seen thirteen hundred English prisoners guarded by eighty Highlanders, I sat down to dine on my bread and cheese and a bottle of Canary wine Mr Seton had made me take at our parting. The remembrance of the glorious and inconceivable victory we had obtained on this spot added to my extreme pleasure at having passed this arm of the sea.

13. Asylum in Leith

As I was afraid of being recognised if I went straight to Edinburgh, I resolved to seek asylum in Leith, in the house of my old governess, Mrs Blythe. She had been twenty-two years in the service of my mother, particularly entrusted with the care of me, having received me from my nurse when I was only twelve months old.

The trouble and uneasiness she had continually experienced on my account, both from the dangerous illnesses to which I had been subject in my youth and from the passionate, impetuous and imprudent character I possessed in common with most only sons, had served merely to increase her kindness and affection for me. She had loved me as if I had been her own child. Mr Blythe, the master of a small coasting vessel, who was very rich, had taken a liking to her when she was fifty, and had offered to marry her. The match had been too advantageous to Margaret for her to hesitate in accepting it. It was three years since she had left our house to reside with her husband at Leith, and they lived very happily together. Blythe was a Calvinist and a sworn enemy of the house of Stuart, but he was a man of much probity and I had nothing to fear from him. I therefore quitted Prestonpans before sunset in order to reach his house in Leith after nightfall.

On entering Mr Blythe's house, I thought the good woman would stifle me with her caresses. She sprang to my neck, clasped me in her arms, and shed a torrent of joyful tears. No one in my family knew what had become of me since the battle of Culloden, whether I was dead or alive, for my brother-in-law, Rollo, had allowed them to remain in ignorance of the fact that he had seen me in Banff. As soon as the first transports of this good woman were over, I entreated her to go instantly to Edinburgh to acquaint my mother and father with the fact that I was in her house and in perfect health. I was the more eager to give them this intelligence as Mrs Blythe had informed me of their great uneasiness and distress on my account. During her absence, Mr Blythe showed me all the hiding places he had caused to be made in the partition of a room – for concealing contraband goods he used to bring in from foreign countries – in order, as he said, that I might take refuge in one of them in the event of surprise and of his house being searched for me. I observed that I was the most contraband and dangerous commodity he had ever had in his possession, and that it was very possible that these hiding places would still prove serviceable, although he had long since concluded that he had no further need of them.

My impatience to give the earliest intelligence to my father had made me neglect to ask Mrs Blythe to bring me clothes, but I had the joy and satisfaction of seeing her return loaded with everything necessary for me. It was indeed time to quit my rags for, besides a thousand other inconveniences to which this disguise had subjected me, I found that they had given me the itch. However, as this disagreeable disease had not yet made much progress, I got rid of it in the course of twenty-four hours by rubbing myself all over with butter and sulphur, and by taking flower of brimstone internally. These rags had been of the greatest use to me during the six weeks I had worn them, but I felt, notwithstanding, an incredible pleasure in throwing them off, and in being no longer obliged to disguise myself as a beggar. My father had sent word that he would call on me in the morning to spend the day with me.

Although I ardently desired to embrace my father, whom I had not seen since the month of October, when our army had left Edinburgh, I nevertheless dreaded this meeting and the reproaches he might make me for having joined Prince Charles without his consent, and for having precipitated myself, by my own fault, into the miserable condition into which I was now plunged. As soon as it had become known in Edinburgh that the Prince had in fact landed in the north-west Highlands, I had been eager to have the merit of being among the first to repair to his banners, staking my fortune on the issue of his cause, and I had earnestly supplicated my father to grant me permission to join him immediately. Instead of granting my request, my father had expressly commanded me to renounce every idea of this nature, telling me that there would be time enough to join the Prince when he was in possession of Edinburgh. He had added that, not being able to procure me a passport, as his principles and attachment to the house of Stuart were universally known, I would be arrested in my attempt to pass the first arm of the sea and kept a prisoner during the whole expedition. In vain I had represented to him that the Prince would look more favourably on me if I joined his standard at the beginning, when he had only a few hundred followers, than when he was in possession of the capital of his ancient Kingdom of Scotland, when the principal obstacles had already been overcome and when he had nothing more to do than be crowned – for this was the light in which I then viewed matters, sadly deceived as I was. My father had been inexorable, and at last he ordered me to be silent.

Burning with desire to join the Prince, I dined the next day with Lady Jane Douglas, who had been my protectress from my infancy, in order to acquaint her with my chagrin and the conversation I had had with my father. This worthy lady highly approved of my reasons, agreed that I ought to set off immediately without further consulting my father, and undertook to appease him should he be enraged at my disobedience. This was precisely the advice I had sought, and I had set out the following morning without saying a word on the subject to anyone.

Experiencing no difficulty in passing the arm of the sea between Queensferry and Dunfermline, I had put a black cockade in my hat and entered the boat with an air of authority, telling those who examined the passports that I was an officer in Lee's regiment, then quartered in Edinburgh, and that officers had no occasion for passports. On leaving the boat I had gone to the castle of Lord Rollo, where I remained for two days awaiting the arrival of the Prince at Perth, two miles thence. When I returned to Edinburgh some time later with our army, my father had said nothing about my going away without his consent, but we were then victorious and triumphant. Now everything was different, and those who had bestowed praise on us in our prosperity treated us, now that we were unfortunate, as hair-brained youths. This is the way with the world in general, who judge of things merely by the event. If we had succeeded in placing the crown on the head of Prince Charles, which had seemed probable for some considerable time, we should all have been celebrated as heroes. The loss of the battle of Culloden, which put an end to the contest between the houses of Stuart and Hanover, made us immediately rebels and madmen in the eyes of those who are incapable of reflection and who, unfortunately, are everywhere in the majority.

My father came to visit me, but instead of reproaching me, the good old man was so affected at seeing me again that his eyes filled with tears and, locking me in his arms, he was for some time unable to utter a single word. As soon as we were a little composed, I amused him with a recital of the particulars of our expedition since our departure from Edinburgh for England, and with all that had happened to me personally since the battle of Culloden. He remained with me until nine o'clock in the evening, and the day passed with the speed of lightning. I was deeply afflicted on learning that my mother was very ill and had been obliged to keep to her room for a long time, and was still more so when Mrs Blythe told me that her anxiety for me was the cause of her illness, and that the physicians thought her life in danger. My grief was natural and well founded, as she had always adored me with the tenderest maternal affection. I proposed several projects to my father for going to see her, but he would not hear of it. He said I would run the risk of being discovered and that, if I should be arrested, it would be the death of both of them. I therefore ceased to insist on seeing her. What a cruel situation, to be so near a mother whom I had such reason for loving tenderly, without being able to embrace her!

Leith, which is about a mile from Edinburgh, was then filled with Hessian and English troops awaiting embarkation for Flanders, and two English sergeants called on Mr Blythe with billets for lodging. This was potentially threatening for me, but Mr Blythe contrived to secure an exemption and they went on their way. For the hour during which the sergeants had remained in the house wrangling with Mr Blythe about lodgings, I watched them continuously through a hole I had made in the partition between two rooms, with entry of a hiding place instantly at hand should I find that they intended to search the house for rebels. I saw poor Mrs Blythe turn pale and change colour every minute, trembling like an aspen leaf, and I was much afraid lest her anxiety should cause the sergeants to suspect that there were rebels concealed in the house. However, my fears were groundless.

I received information that Lady Jane Douglas intended to pay me a visit *incognito* on the afternoon of the following day, accompanied by Mr Stewart, who later became her husband, and another lady who was related to me. The worthy and virtuous Lady Jane, who was idolised by her country, possessed every good and amiable quality that could adorn her sex. She was beloved, respected and adored by all those who had the advantage of knowing her, as well as by the public in general, who knew her only by the reputation of the high character she possessed. She had been very beautiful in her youth, and was still beautiful at the age of forty-five, appearing at least fifteen years younger than she really was, from the uniform, temperate, regular, frugal and simple way of life she had always observed. She was virtuous, pious, devout, charitable and without ostentation, and her devoutness was neither affected nor oppressive to others. Her affability, her easy, engaging manners, and her goodness of heart soon set at ease those who paid court to her, whom her graceful and majestic air might at first have rendered timid. Her mind was highly cultivated. She had a decided taste for literature, a great memory, much good sense and intelligence, sound judgment, and quick discernment. Her library was well stocked with the best authors, without any of those trifling novels that generally form so large a portion of the libraries of some women. She possessed great elevation of the soul, and was even haughty and proud on proper occasions, supporting her illustrious birth with dignity yet without arrogance or vanity, in a manner truly noble.

Her brother, the Duke of Douglas, had been a lunatic from his infancy, frequently breaking out into the most dreadful fits of madness. He had killed his own near relation, Mr Ker, without ever having had the least quarrel or altercation with him, by running him through the body with his sword while he was asleep. As Lady Jane herself several times narrowly escaped being killed by him in fits of insanity, their uncle, the Marquis of Lothian, had wished to have him legally declared a lunatic and to have Lady Jane put in possession of all the estates of the family, amounting to more than sixteen thousand pounds a year. This would have met with no opposition, as his lunacy was notorious from the fatal proofs of it he gave daily, but Lady Jane would not hear of it, preferring to live retired on an annuity of three or four hundred a year, which she drew from her brother as interest on her portion – a very small income for a person of her rank – rather than dishonour him and her family by having recourse to such a step. If ever virtue seemed to be unceasingly persecuted by Providence, it was in the person of Lady Jane Douglas, the most amiable of her sex, eminent for every noble quality, and the most perfect model for imitation.

Lady Jane called on me, as she had announced, and made me repeat all my adventures since the battle of Culloden. When I came to tell her of my stay at Samuel's, I recalled my dream – which I had almost forgotten amid the vicissitudes experienced since leaving Glen-Prossen – and, struck with its force in every point and circumstance, I stopped short for a moment in my narrative, remaining silent and confounded. I hesitated at first as to whether I should describe it or not, but it seemed so supernatural and incredible that I was afraid to communicate it to her, lest she should think I was regaling her with fiction. Besides, supposing that she would not believe me, which seemed highly probable, it would have appeared to her eyes – so I thought – to betray smallness of mind, an attempt to deceive her by artifice. I therefore proceeded with my story, omitting all account of my dream, although nothing can be more certain than that, by inspiring me with an obstinate determination to proceed south instead of returning to the mountains to join my companions, this dream actually saved my life. I shall therefore remember it, for as long as I live, as a matter beyond my comprehension and powers of reason, although it had such a decisive influence on my destiny.

Having recounted to Lady Jane the affair of the two sergeants on the preceding evening which had so alarmed poor Mrs Blythe, she observed that I was not then in a suitable place, and offered me asylum in her house, where I should be safer, as no one would dare search it on mere suspicion. She told me to come that very night at about ten o'clock, and ordered me to collect my rags for the journey. Her house was about half a league from Leith, in the village of Drumsheugh, and the disguise was absolutely necessary lest I meet anyone on the way who knew me. I said all I possibly could to avoid having to wear my old clothes, for which I entertained a particular repugnance, but, as I durst not tell Lady Jane that they had given me the itch, I was obliged to wear them in order to comply with her request. I took every possible precaution to avoid catching that odious disease a second time, wearing two shirts, a waistcoat and gloves under my rags.

14. Sanctuary with Lady Jane

I arrived at the door of Lady Jane's house at about eleven o'clock that night, and found it half-open. Her gardener, the only servant she dared entrust with the secret, was waiting for me. He told me that Lady Jane had ordered him to conduct me into her apartment as soon as I arrived, without changing my clothes, as she wished to see me in my disguise. This was another source of uneasiness, for I dreaded the pestilential odour with which they would fill the room, but I had no alternative. I found Lady Jane, Mr Stewart and a lady who was related to me waiting to see my metamorphosis. They all agreed that it was impossible to recognise me in this dress, although Lady Jane observed that, to complete the disguise, I ought to have blackened my eyebrows with burnt cork. I tried the experiment immediately, and found that it produced a considerable alteration in my appearance. I took my leave of them at about midnight, and was conducted by the gardener to the chamber designated for me, above the room where company was received and where no one had slept for a long time past. I made a bundle of my clothes, and immediately asked the gardener to burn them in the garden, that I might hear no more of them and be under no apprehension of ever having to wear them again.

As the gardener was the only person in on the secret, and as all the servants imagined that there was no one in the room I occupied, I was obliged, so as not to attract attention which might lead to my discovery, to remain without shoes until eleven o'clock at night, when they went to bed. This was the earliest I was able to go downstairs to take a walk in the garden. I soon became accustomed to this sedentary, secluded life, seldom seeing anyone but the gardener, who brought me my meals. I sometimes had the pleasure of passing a few hours in the apartment of Lady Jane, where I usually found Mr Stewart, but this was an indulgence I seldom enjoyed on account of the difficulty of keeping servants out of the way, especially the chambermaid, Mrs Ker. Lady Jane did not wish to let this woman in on the secret, and she became very troublesome from her extreme curiosity to clear up the mystery, the existence of which she had frequent occasion to suspect without knowing what to make of it.

I immediately acquired a taste for reading, having been until then too dissipated for any application to books, and her Ladyship supplied me with the best historical authors. Thus I passed most of my time there with a book in my hand, without feeling weariness for a single moment, and I should have willingly consented to pass my whole life in this manner on condition of escaping the scaffold. The taste for reading which I then acquired has subsequently been of the greatest utility to me, a great resource against *ennui* in a part of America where I lived for several years and where society was not as agreeable as in Europe.

A few days after taking possession of my lodgings in the house of Lady Jane, I read in an Edinburgh newspaper 'that the populace of Dubbieside had arrested and conducted to prison a person by the name of David Cousselain, who, with a certain individual who was not taken, had aided in the escape of a rebel, and that they had burnt the boat, which had been used in crossing the ferry'. I was very glad that Seton, who had acted with such generosity, had had the good fortune to escape, and I was sorry that Mr Robertson had lost his boat. As to Cousselain, I could not pity his fate as much as if he had kept himself sober, for my hands were not yet healed. Had it not been for his drunkenness, he might have returned to Dubbieside in better time for, had we been able to relieve each other, we should have effected our passage in far less time. There was therefore every reason for supposing that he might have escaped being taken, by securing his return before the inhabitants were awake, if he had remained sober. I had rowed as well as a man could do who was rowing for his life without much experience of the business, but with Cousselain we should have effected the passage in half the time. I learned from Mr Seton the elder, whom I met in Paris in 1747, that Cousselain suffered only a few weeks' imprisonment as there was no evidence against him. Indeed, nothing would have been more unjust than to have condemned him for saving a rebel, for the brute had had nothing to do with it, having slept during the whole crossing while I fatigued myself to death with rowing, injuring my hands in such a way as to prevent me from using them for a long time afterwards.

Lady Jane and my father were of the opinion that I should go immediately to London, as I ran no risk of being discovered in that immense city which multitudes of strangers were entering and leaving every day. They thought, too, that there would be little to fear on the road once I was ten leagues distant from Edinburgh. Everything was ready for my departure when we learned that the squadron of the Duke d'Anville had sailed from France, and that it was so formidable that Admiral Anson dared not attack it. When this news first reached Scotland, no one doubted that this squadron was destined to re-establish the affairs of Prince Charles, and the feigned route – as we thought – it had taken on its departure confirmed us still more in that belief. It is certain that this squadron might have effected a disembarkation in Scotland without encountering the least opposition, even in the view of the English fleets which had dared not attack it. The troops on board would have been more than sufficient to re-establish our affairs, and the Scots who were concealed in the mountains would have issued

out of them like so many bees from a hive. Many of the
clans who had remained neutral, seeing that the Duke of
Cumberland had ravaged and laid waste the whole country
without distinction between friend or foe, would have taken
up arms. The army of the Prince would soon have been
double, in number, what it had been in the times of our
greatest prosperity. After waiting with extreme impatience
for the landing of this squadron in Scotland, which occupied
the attention of everyone for several weeks, an English ship
at length discovered it in a latitude which placed beyond
doubt the fact that it was destined for America.

It was the fate of this formidable fleet to perish on the
coast of Nova Scotia, without even effecting the settlement
which was the object of the expedition at Chebuctoo, a paltry
fort in the worst possible soil, where the English have since
built the town of Halifax. This immense armament, which
might easily have effected a revolution in England from the
critical state of things at that time in Scotland, was reduced to
nothing by tempests, disease, discord and contention between
the superior officers of the land and sea services – in short,
by a total want of good conduct, so that only a few shattered
remains returned to France. This may be considered as the
last effort of the French navy.

The policy pursued by the court of France, in threatening
the English with efforts in the cause of the house of Stuart,
as they have done for a century past, was very short-
sighted. In the nature of things, this policy could only be
of limited operation. The trick had become so stale from
repetition that the English were no longer alarmed by it,
as they saw that France, with the best possible dispositions,
had become incapable of effecting anything in favour of the
Stuarts because of the destruction and emigration of their
partisans in Scotland, and the coolness of those in England.

This was indeed clearly proved in the last war.[1] These pretended invasions in no manner disconcerted the English or prevented them from pursuing their enterprises, and only served to open their eyes to the necessity of forming and disciplining a hundred thousand militia to guard their coasts from surprise. If France had seriously desired to re-establish the house of Stuart on the throne, she might easily have succeeded in effecting this during our expedition with three or four thousand troops. Having an ally in Prince Charles, she would thereby have avoided those eternal wars with England which had never taken place during the reign of the house of Stuart. On the contrary, Charles II had been an ally of France in a war against the Dutch, notwithstanding the friendly sentiments the English had always entertained towards that republic.

After passing two months in the house of Lady Jane Douglas in the most tranquil and philosophical manner, a maid-servant who had returned from Edinburgh with provisions told her companions in the kitchen that, while she was purchasing meat in the flesh-market, the lackey of an English gentleman, a commissioner of the customs, had whispered in her ear 'that they knew very well that I was concealed in the house of Lady Jane Douglas, her mistress, and that there was every reason for supposing that her house would immediately be searched'. She added that she had openly contradicted this calumny – and in fact she could do so with a safe conscience, for no one in the house except the gardener knew anything of the matter. The gardener immediately went upstairs to inform Lady Jane, who came into my room without delay, accompanied by Mr Stewart, to consult as to what needed to be done, fearing lest a

[1] The Seven Years War (1756-1763).

detachment of soldiers should come in the course of the day to visit the house. It was then only nine o'clock in the morning.

This intelligence filled me with the utmost grief and unease. I trembled lest the extreme goodness of Lady Jane in giving me asylum should involve her in difficulties with the government, and I was a thousand times more afraid of the disagreeable consequences my being taken in her house would entail for her than of the fate that would await me. When I feelingly expressed how much I regretted the danger to which I had exposed her, she replied with her usual spirit and promptitude: 'If there were no risk, you'd be under no obligation to me.'

It was impossible to go out by the door into the courtyard, on account of the servants who would see me from the kitchen, and there was no place in the house – which I had examined all over – where I could remain concealed. But as they were then making hay in an enclosure belonging to Lady Jane, Mr Stewart proposed that I should conceal myself in a cock of hay. In order to succeed in this, it was necessary to let a footman into the secret, that he might watch the other servants and seize a favourable opportunity for me to leave the house in order to enter the enclosure.

I went out in my waistcoat with the footman and the gardener, followed by Mr Stewart. As it was necessary to observe a number of precautions, on account of some of the windows of the village which overlooked the enclosure, we began to throw down all the cocks of hay, one after another, and the footman and the gardener threw each other down on the hay, at which the one who happened to be the undermost was covered by the other. This pretended amusement went on for some time until they threw me down, in my turn, as part of the same sport, and covered me with hay until the cock in which I was concealed was raised as high as the rest, leaving me only a small aperture for breathing. Then, having given me a bottle of water and another of wine, they withdrew.

I do not think it was possible for me to suffer more than I did that whole day. The weather was fine but very warm, and the excessive heat of my situation under the hay, which was like an oven, almost deprived me of respiration. Mr Stewart came to see me from time to time, and exhorted me to be patient. Indeed I had need of patience, for my sufferings were at times so unbearable that I was tempted to give the hay to the devil and expose myself to whatever might happen rather than continue where I was. My regard for Lady Jane alone restrained me. After the most dreadful sufferings from ten o'clock in the morning until nine at night, remaining always in the same attitude without power to stir myself, and bathed in sweat, I was at length relieved. When I came out of the hay, my body was so bruised and I was so weak from excessive transpiration that I could only walk with difficulty, leaning on the arm of Mr Stewart, for my legs could scarcely support me. I was enraged to think I had passed so disagreeable a day for nothing, no person having come to search the house. I was always of the opinion that they would not dare do so on doubtful information, and they could have obtained no certain information otherwise than through the gardener, of whose fidelity Lady Jane had been assured throughout the considerable time he had been in her service.

The eventual certainty that the squadron of the Duke d'Anville was not destined for Scotland, the consequent disappointment I felt at the extinction of all my hopes for the re-establishment of our affairs, and my sufferings the whole of this day under the hay, all determined me to set out for London as soon as possible. Mr Colville, Lady Jane's man of business, purchased for me the next day in the horse-market a very handsome pony at a reasonable price. I urgently entreated Lady Jane to exempt me from performing a second penance during the day I would still have the honour of spending with her, adding that I would remain sentinel at my chamber window from morning to night, my eyes constantly fixed on the door into the courtyard. As soon as I saw a detachment enter – if they were so imprudent as to send one – I would jump from the window of the first floor into the garden whence, by climbing the garden wall, I could soon gain the open fields and place myself beyond the reach of their pursuit. This dear and amiable lady pitied my suffering under the haycock but, at the same time, could not help bursting into a loud fit of laughter on seeing my panic-terror at the idea of returning to it, and she granted me the dispensation requested.

The next day my father came to bid me an eternal *adieu*, and spent the afternoon with me. I felt the utmost affliction and grief at the approach of this perpetual separation, and I warmly urged my father, as well as Lady Jane, to permit me to go to Edinburgh for a few moments to embrace for the last time the most tender and affectionate of mothers in the bed where she was then dangerously ill. They would not, however, give their consent on account of the danger of my being discovered, either in passing through the town or by the servants of the house. What a cruel situation, to be within a mile of the tenderest mother, then dangerously ill, who had always fondly loved me, and yet being unable to bid her an eternal *adieu*.

At about eleven o'clock that night, I disguised myself in the dress of one of the persons who travel up and down the country with goods. There was procured for me a stock of handkerchiefs, which I put with my linen into a portmanteau where I also had a very beautiful embroidered waistcoat, which was very precious to me as it was the work of a mistress. Having folded up my hair, I put on a black wig that hung down over my shoulders, and Lady Jane blackened my eyebrows, although I was by no means as completely metamorphosed by this disguise as I had been by my disguise as a beggar. The amiable Lady Jane, who could not be at ease on my account until she knew I had proceeded some leagues from Edinburgh without incident, sent a servant on her saddle-horse to accompany me for the first two leagues, that she might know how I had progressed. I should then be less exposed to meet anyone of my acquaintance than in the neighbourhood of that city.

15. Southern Suspicions

I had travelled about six leagues without stopping when, having come to a village in which there was a public house, I dismounted to rest a while and take some refreshment. The landlady eagerly pressed me to join a gentleman, who had just arrived, in the next room, that we might dine together. I consented, thinking that she was unable to serve us dinner separately. I was confounded, on entering the room, to find Mr Scott, a young gentleman who was a banker in Edinburgh and who knew me very well by sight. This encounter was the more calculated to alarm me because he was a violent partisan of the house of Hanover. Having committed this blunder, however, it was too late to retreat. Trusting to my disguise, I supported the character of a pedlar as best I could until, in a moment of absence, Mr Scott pronounced my name. As it was impossible to doubt any longer that I was recognised, I endeavoured to deceive him as to the road I intended to take. As several roads joined the highway to Edinburgh at this village, I told him I intended sleeping at Jedburgh, the road to which turned off from the London road on the right at this village. After he had spoken my name, I noticed that Mr Scott was at great pains to give the impression that he did not know me, the motive for which I was unable to discover. I was not afraid of being arrested in the village, having a pistol primed and loaded in each breeches pocket, but I was very much afraid that, on reaching Edinburgh in the evening, this individual would lodge an information against me and that, in consequence, the magistrates of the different towns on the London road would be instructed to arrest me.

I therefore set out immediately after dinner, taking at first the Jedburgh road, but, as soon as I had proceeded about a league, turning left at a crossroad and soon regaining the

London road. That evening I arrived at Kelso, forty-three miles from Edinburgh. There, availing myself of a letter of recommendation from Mr Stewart, I slept at a private house to avoid any troublesome encounters at the inn. I never passed a more painful day. Plunged into the deepest melancholy and oppressed with the most distressing reflections, I saw myself reduced to the dreadful alternatives of perishing on the scaffold or – by escaping to a foreign country – abandoning forever my native land, my relations, my friends, and all that was dear to me.

The next day I crossed over into England.

On the fourth day after my departure from Edinburgh, within two miles of Stamford, where I intended spending the night, I suddenly caught up with some covered waggons. I heard a voice call out from within one of the waggons: 'See, see if there is not a man on horseback who resembles our rebel captain as much as one drop of water resembles another,' and I heard my name pronounced in the same breath.

Among the immense number of prisoners we had taken in the different battles we had gained against the English, there were many who had entered our army without any sincerity of purpose. Most of them had had no other objective in mind than obtaining the means of later escaping, with greater ease, to rejoin their old colours in the English army.

I had been informed, while in the house of Lady Jane Douglas, that several waggons, filled with soldiers wounded at the battle of Culloden, had set off for Chelsea Hospital, near London, about eight days before I had left Edinburgh. I had supposed that they would be too far ahead of me for there to be any danger of me catching up with them on my way. Not expecting to meet any person in England who knew me, I had taken off my large black wig on account of the excessive heat, and had only my hat, uncocked, covering my face as if to protect me from the sun. I affected not to hear them and, having passed the waggons, I kept on at the same pace until I got clear of the town of Stamford, when I put spurs to my horse and rode eight miles at full gallop to get sufficiently far in front of the soldiers that they would not see me again. I dared not sleep at Stamford, as I was afraid that their report might induce the magistrates to arrest me.

This adventure nearly proved fatal for my horse, the loss of which would have reduced me to so grievous a situation that I trembled at the very thought of it. On reaching the inn where I decided to sleep, my horse he threw himself down as soon as he entered the stable, refusing to eat or drink, and seemed to be completely done in. I tortured my imagination to think how I could continue my journey in the event of my horse being incapable of proceeding further. I also dreaded the arrival of the waggons, the next morning, at that very inn, which was the only one in the village. Restless and chagrined beyond all description, I did nothing but pace to and fro between the inn and the stable for about two hours. At length, after inexpressible suffering, I was agreeably surprised to find my horse once more on his legs, eating heartily and looking healthy. The landlord told me I had nothing to fear, and even offered to buy my horse at thrice the price he had cost me. Nothing could exceed the joy I felt in having my mind thus set at ease concerning my horse, the recovery of which extricated me from the cruellest perplexity. The landlord added that in a few hours the animal would feel nothing more of his fatigue, and that I might set off with him in the morning at any hour I pleased without the least danger of him failing me on the way. I fixed my departure for half-past two in the morning, on the pretext of avoiding the heat, but in reality to stay ahead of the waggons, for they weighed heavily on my mind.

The next morning, at sunrise, a man very well dressed in the manner of the people, about forty years of age and mounted on a very beautiful bay courser, came across the fields, leaping all the hedges and ditches with astonishing facility. As soon as he entered the highway, he came alongside me and immediately tried to start a conversation notwithstanding my disinclination to co-operate, which he could easily judge from my monosyllabic answers. Having examined his physiognomy when he rode up on my left, I observed that he had a wild and troubled air, and that he constantly turned his head to look about him in all directions. In short, he gave every impression of being one of those highwaymen with whom the great roads of England are infested. I kept my right hand in my beeches pocket and, while I held my pistol in readiness, I kept my eyes ever fixed on him, determined that if he made the least movement with his hands, my pistol would be presented as soon as his. I likewise regulated the pace of my horse by his, never allowing him to get behind me, which I perceived he sometimes wished to do from the constant slackening of his pace. I did not wish to surrender my purse without a battle as, in my situation, the loss of the money I had with me would have ruined me irretrievably.

Having proceeded in this manner for more than half an hour, always on alert and making a number of seemingly unconnected observations, the stranger suddenly wished me good morning and darted, in the same manner as he had come, across the fields, leaping the hedges and ditches without appearing to have any object in view other than gaining as great a distance as possible from the highway. The determined air I had exhibited probably deterred him from demanding my purse, and I was very glad to be rid of him, for the adventure, however it may have turned out, could have proved fatal to me. If I had blown out his brains in my own defence, I could not have presented myself before a magistrate to make my deposition; and if he had taken my purse, I know not how I would have continued my journey without money.

While I was dining in an inn at Jockey Houses, a man entered whom I took, from his conversation with the landlord, to be an excise officer. This man rudely seated himself at my table without the least apology and without asking my leave. He remained a quarter of an hour without speaking, during which time he made a considerable breach in a piece of roasted veal. At length, unable to devour more, he laid down his knife and fork with much gravity and said to me with an air of contented satisfaction: 'Sir, I saw you pass this morning; you probably slept at Stamford? I perceived at once from your horse – for we have none of that breed in England – that you are come from Scotland. Tell me whether it be true that the rebels are entirely dispersed? It must be owned that your nation is very eager for its own destruction. Have we ever been governed with so much mildness and moderation as at present under His Majesty King George? Your nation will never be quiet until it be totally destroyed. Can nothing extirpate in your country that hereditary spirit of rebellion?'

I was very uneasy, fearing that this rude fellow had been sent by the magistrates of Stamford to verify the declaration of the soldiers, with instructions to keep sight of me until he should find an opportunity to arrest me in the first large town where I might spend the night. I answered that I had no news of the rebels, having come from a part of the country called Annandale, which is on the frontier of England and where they generally know little or nothing of what is passing in the north of Scotland. Besides, being a dealer in linen drapery, I concerned myself only with my trade and cared very little about affairs of state.

He immediately asked to see my goods. I told him I had sent my linen to London by sea with other goods of Scots manufacture, and that I had only handkerchiefs with me. I immediately opened my portmanteau to show him, and sold him a piece without knowing the price, as they had forgotten to mark it. I had not, it is true, anticipated any such embarrassment on the road to London as would oblige me to sell them. On paying for the handkerchiefs, he praised my probity, telling me that I was a conscientious young man and that all the other Scots pedlars who daily passed along this road were a set of arrant knaves, having lately obliged him to pay, for the same goods, nearly the double what I had asked. In examining my portmanteau, he saw my embroidered waistcoat and expressed a strong desire to purchase it, but as soon as I told him that I could not sell it for less than fifteen guineas he gave up all idea of buying it, and I was very glad that he did not torment me further, for I should not have let him have it on any account. If this man really had been sent after me, as I suspected, he must at least have reported that I was a pedlar, and that the handkerchiefs I had sold him, apparently for less than cost, had given him a high opinion of my honesty. He made me take down the addresses of his friends in London, in order that they might obtain similar goods from me at the same price.

16. Love Affair in London

I arrived in London at six o'clock in the evening on the seventh day after my departure from Lady Jane Douglas's house, having travelled nearly four hundred miles without over-fatiguing my horse. I alighted at an inn in Greek Street, the people of which Mr Stewart had recommended to me as honest and well behaved. As soon as I had changed my linen, I went out to deliver a letter of recommendation to a person from whom the only favour I had to ask was to procure me furnished lodgings to which I might immediately proceed, in order to avoid the inconvenience of sleeping at an inn. Having found him at home, he declined – to my great surprise – to procure lodgings for me, telling me at the same time that, the master of the inn being a Scotsman much suspected by the government, it was generally supposed that the court employed some of his waiters as spies, to give them intelligence of all the Scotsmen arriving in London. I returned to the inn highly incensed at the rudeness of this person who would not trouble himself to find me lodgings, and I was very uneasy, after what I had heard, at being obliged to spend the night there.

I did not close an eye that whole night from fear of being arrested on the information of spies at the inn. Rising at an early hour the next day, I went out in quest of furnished lodgings, without being able to find any in a neighbourhood that suited my pocket. Impatient and anxious to quit the inn, I at length bethought me of a woman who kept a shop, and who had had a great kindness for me when I had been in London in 1740. All I had to do was ascertain whether she had adopted anyone in my place whom she loved better than me, or whether, after an absence of five years, I could revive the affection I had formerly inspired in her. However, as she possessed good sense, elevated sentiments and great gentleness of disposition,

I felt sure that I ran no risk in confiding my life to her fidelity, and I therefore immediately took a coach and drove to her house. Having dismissed the coach some distance from the door, I entered her shop on the pretext of buying something, supposing that she would not recognise me, but she no sooner saw me than she called me by name in a transport of joy at seeing me again. As her maid-servant was present, I told her that she had forgotten my name, which was Leslie. We then entered the parlour, where I told her of my misfortunes, drawing tears from her eyes, and I soon saw that this good and amiable woman still loved me. I told her that the convincing proof I had received from her of her friendship and affection made me believe that my life was safe in her hands. 'Oh yes,' she replied, with great vivacity. She then embraced me, and entreated me to be assured that she loved me as much as ever, and that she had often thought of me.

She immediately offered me an apartment in her house, telling me that I would be the more safe with her as she had never let her apartments, and she pressed me enthusiastically to take the lodging in question without delay. I accepted her obliging offer, returned to the inn for my portmanteau, and came back to dine with her. She gave me an elegant front room on the first floor. Having found a stable in the neighbourhood, I brought my horse to it myself that evening, so that the people of the inn, if they were spies of the court, might not know where I had taken up lodgings. I ceased, therefore, to be uneasy on that score.

My horse was so handsome that I sold him almost immediately on such advantageous terms that I received, over and above the price I had paid for him, much more than the expense of my journey and my loss on the handkerchiefs.

I had formerly lived in London for a year, in consequence of a dispute with my father, until I received an order from him in the spring of 1740 to return to Scotland. He allowed me only three weeks to return to him, on pain of his never pardoning my disobedience. I was in this critical situation when, on a visit I paid to one of my friends to announce my departure, I had met in his house the most beautiful person who ever existed, eighteen years of age, newly come from the country. She was the niece of my friend, and an only daughter. I stopped to dine at her uncle's, where she stayed, and her engaging manners, sweet air, and conversation seasoned with good sense, wit and modesty, without the least tincture of affectation, conspired with her beauty to captivate me and make me feel with violence the torment of a growing passion. I had never felt anything like this before. I had often, indeed, been in love, but it had been that easy kind of love we lose, without knowing how or why, when a short absence or the presence of another beauty dissolves the charm and makes us quickly forget the fair one for whom we sighed. But this charming person had placed me in a dreadful situation. I was bewildered and no longer knew myself. I had not spoken to her of my departure, although it had been the subject of my visit, and her uncle had invited me to pass the day after the next with them.

I had remained in London adoring this divine beauty until I had no more money than was barely sufficient to defray the expenses of my journey to Scotland. Then, struggling continuously between love and duty, I suddenly decided to set off the next morning without taking my leave, mainly from a distrust of my self-command and an internal conviction that a single glance at the charming Miss Peggy would instantly overturn my resolutions, however wise and prudent they might be. I feared that on seeing her I would no longer be the master of myself, and would become entangled in fresh embarrassments. I had arrived at my father's, a reconciliation had immediately taken place, and the past had been forgotten.

During the six years I had remained in Scotland at a distance from the adorable Peggy, the uncertainty of her feelings for me, the little hope I had of seeing her again, time, which effaces everything, and new objects, though of inferior beauty – all conspired to make me insensibly forget her. But the moment I returned to London, her image immediately presented itself to my mind. My passion rekindled itself to such a flame that the certainty of the consequence of a visit being death on the scaffold would not have prevented me from attempting to see her again. I delayed my visit only until the clothes I had ordered were ready, and my tailor accommodated my impatience by bringing them, with my beautiful embroidered waistcoat, within twenty-four hours.

As soon as I was dressed I took a hackney coach, which I discharged when I was near her uncle's, and enquired of the servant who opened the door if his master was at home. He replied that he was not, but that he was expected for dinner. I then enquired whether his niece, Miss Peggy, was in town or in the country. The plain answer of the servant that she was 'in the house' gave me such a palpitation of the heart, and such a trembling in my nerves, that I could scarcely stand upright. I stepped into the parlour and sent the servant to ask if she were visible. He immediately returned to announce that she was coming down. The presence of this charming person, who appeared before my eyes more beautiful than ever, increased my disorder, and I remained motionless as a statue. In vain I attempted to speak. My mouth and tongue refused to perform their functions. As soon as I was sufficiently tranquillised, I told her that, having been engaged in the unfortunate affair of Prince Charles, I had hesitated very much whether or not I should present myself to her uncle lest I expose him to disagreeable consequences in the event that I were discovered in his house. But the remembrance of the civilities and kindness I had received from him six years before had been so deeply engraved on my mind that I could not resist the temptation of personally offering him the assurance of my lasting gratitude.

While I spoke, the adorable Miss Peggy looked at me with eyes full of compassion, pity and sweetness, and said that her uncle, having always entertained a sincere friendship for me, would certainly feel for my misfortunes, and that he would disregard any inconvenience to which he might expose himself for the pleasure of seeing me and of being useful to me. In the meantime her uncle entered, and was very surprised to see me again. He embraced me affectionately, and when I related my disasters to him, he replied that I was a pretty fellow to wish to be a king-maker and that, for his part, he did not care whether King George, King James or the devil himself were on the throne of England, provided he was left in peaceable possession of his estates, which he would not hazard for all the kings in the universe. He added that he felt very much for my situation, and advised me to shun all places where I might meet any of my countrymen. He made a hearty offer of his house until I could find an opportunity of escaping beyond the sea, and begged me to avail myself of his offer immediately by remaining to dine with them.

Several persons called on them after dinner, to whom the uncle introduced me under the name of Mr Leslie, and I made a party at quadrille with Miss Peggy and two other ladies. How quickly does time glide by in the company of those we love! I passed with her the whole of the most delicious day I had ever known, which appeared to me but an instant. The uncle told me at supper that he had stayed at home all afternoon on my account, and begged me to have the goodness to lay aside all ceremony as he no longer considered me a stranger in his house. I returned to pass the night in the house of my generous woman friend with a quiet, contented mind, but before taking my leave, the uncle invited me to come every day to breakfast, and to pass the day with them. His adorable niece joined in the invitation, adding that by going out early in the morning I should be less exposed to meet in the streets any of my countrymen who might happen to know me. He likewise offered me a room in his house, which I chose not to accept for fear of involving him in some awkward affair should I be followed in the streets by anyone who knew me, and arrested in his house.

I passed fifteen days constantly with the adorable Peggy from nine o'clock in the morning until eleven o'clock at night. I had not yet dared declare to her that I loved her, for fear of shocking her. How timid we are when we love sincerely! What a change in my character! I no longer knew myself. I had always been bold and enterprising with the fair sex, and when I did not succeed I made my retreat with good grace and without being disconcerted. But in the presence of this divine person, I looked down when she turned her eyes towards me, and whenever I attempted to reveal my passion I immediately began to tremble. She seemed to me a supreme good that I was afraid of losing, in case her feelings towards me were unfavourable. Always afraid of offending her, by even the slightest word, I allowed no sign of my excessive love and affection to escape me other than an occasional sigh, or an apparent uneasiness, which she might very well attribute to my unfortunate situation and not to the true cause.

Having passed a whole day *tête-à-tête* with her, I at length threw myself suddenly at her feet, seized her hands in a transport, and bathed them with my tears. I could only say, with a broken voice and trembling lips, that I adored her and that I wished to live only for her. She immediately asked me to rise, telling me coolly that she had always held me in great esteem, that she was extremely sorry to see me in the terrible crisis in which I found myself, poised between life and death, that every day my companions were dragged to the scaffold, and that I might at any moment expect to follow them in order to undergo the same punishment. She exhorted me to think more rationally, and to consider the means of saving my life rather than filling my head with chimeras. But from that moment on, I had tacit permission to express all the tenderness and affection the most violent passion could inspire, which however never failed to elicit from her strong reprimands and advice to act more like a reasonable man.

Her cold and reserved behaviour towards me grieved and affected me beyond all endurance, while her gracious, prepossessing and engaging manners towards other men, whom she treated so differently, rendered me excessively jealous. I imagined that all those to whom she showed the least civility or politeness stood much higher in her opinion, and were much more in her good graces, than I was. One of her relations had made her a present of a handsome snuffbox of *ecaille tournée de Maubois*, lined with gold and an exquisitely beautiful miniature, one of the first of these boxes to appear in England. One day when I was *tête-à-tête* with her, she seemed to me absent and thoughtful, frequently taking out the box and examining the miniature. My jealousy instantly broke out against the box. I bitterly reproached her, observing that her mind could certainly not be occupied with the miniature, which she had so often seen, but with the person who had made her a present of it; that he was the happiest of mortals in possessing her heart, whilst my cruel and sad fate was truly pitiable; that I was overwhelmed with afflictions of every kind and ready to sink under my misfortunes; that I could support with patience her rigours and the cold indifference she continually showed me, but that the thought of her loving another, and of my having a happy rival, plunged a dagger into my heart. The adorable Peggy immediately dashed the snuffbox against the marble chimneypiece, which broke it into a thousand pieces, telling me with warmth that I should never have any reason to fear a rival, that she loved me tenderly, and that she would no longer conceal her feelings towards me. She conjured me at the same time to take no improper advantage of this knowledge, and to be satisfied with her friendship, which would be constant and invariable as long as she lived.

One day, hearing from my room a noise in the street, I approached the window and was shocked to see twelve of my companions being led to Kennington Common for execution on the scaffold. They belonged to the garrison Prince Charles had left behind at Carlisle on our retreat from England, and Messrs Hamilton and Townley, the governors of the town and castle of Carlisle, were amongst this unfortunate party. I was the more struck on seeing them because, had it not been for my obstinacy and firmness, I should probably be undergoing this ignominious punishment along with them. When the Duke of Perth, my colonel, had commanded me, on our retreat, to remain with my company in Carlisle, I had answered that I would willingly shed the last drop of my blood for Prince Charles, but that I would not allow myself to be marked out as a victim for certain destruction, and I had left him in a rage without waiting for his reply. Persisting in my resolution, I had set out the next morning with our army. Two days after our departure, when news of the capture of Carlisle by the Duke of Cumberland reached us, the Duke of Perth, who was of very limited capacity, but at the same time a most worthy and gallant man, told me that he pardoned my disobedience, and that he had been deceived as to the strength of the place, as he had believed it capable of sustaining a siege. I fervently thanked the Almighty who had watched over my destiny, for, without my obstinacy, my lot at that moment would have been to end my days in the same fatal manner.

The lack of attention I paid to my hospitable woman friend, with whom I lodged, began somewhat to irritate her, render her uneasy, and even sour her disposition towards me. In reality she had every reason to be angry with me, as I passed all of my time with the adorable Peggy, and when absent from her I was thoughtful, lost in reverie, and incapable of showing my hostess the gratitude she amply deserved for the essential services she had rendered me. She frequently reproached me for my coldness and indifference, and I pitied her myself, for she truly was a woman who deserved greater attention from me for the continual kindness she showed me, and for the warm and tender interest she took in everything to do with me. I always blamed my cruel fate as the cause, and endeavoured to persuade her of the impossibility of my being otherwise, suspended as I then was between life and death, seeing my companions daily led to the scaffold, and uncertain as to whether I should not immediately follow them. This good and amiable woman possessed great sweetness and good sense, and was sufficiently well disposed to believe whatever I told her.

While I was breakfasting one morning in my room with my landlady, I was thunderstruck at seeing the adorable Peggy enter, excited by a desire to see my landlady, for some distrust she entertained with respect to me. My poor landlady, the moment she saw the angelic Peggy, fixed her eyes on the ground, blushed, and was quite confounded. She wished to withdraw, but I prevented her. Peggy, having satisfied her curiosity, left after about a quarter of an hour and whispered in my ear, on going downstairs, that she had nothing to fear. My landlady immediately reproached me, but without bitterness, observing that she was no longer astonished at my indifference, now that she had seen the cause of it; that she could not blame me, as the lady was the most beautiful person she had ever seen, with the most engaging manners and an affable air full of goodness; and she added that she was certain no man could resist her charms. I wished to avail myself of the same arguments I had urged before, but she was no longer to be duped by them.

Whatever confidence I might have had in the sweetness and honourable disposition of my landlady, it was nevertheless prudent to take precaution against the possible negative effect of this adventure, especially as she might, in a moment of irritation, be tempted to have recourse to vengeance. All she had to do was to inform against me, and I would be instantly arrested. The resentment of women who suppose themselves slighted has all too frequently displayed itself in this manner. I therefore resolved to look for other lodgings that very day, and I was fortunate to find an apartment in the house of a hairdresser in the neighbourhood of the mansion of my dear Peggy. Having told my landlady the next morning that I had found an opportunity of effecting my escape beyond sea, I immediately quitted my lodgings, after taking leave of this amiable woman and giving her all possible assurance of my gratitude and my eternal remembrance for the services she had rendered me. She embraced me with tears in her eyes, truly affected by our parting, and as my heart was not sufficiently hard to resist a beautiful woman in tears, I was very sensibly touched by her sentiments for me.

One day, on returning from an evening walk, having learned that one of my relations had arrived from Scotland, I told Peggy of my anxiety to obtain news of my family and, instead of supping with her as usual, I took a coach and drove to the lodgings of my relation. As soon as I entered he began to condole with me on the loss I had sustained, but I paid no particular attention, imagining that he was referring to the misfortunes that were common to all who had been attached to Prince Charles, including me. However, he soon gave me to understand that my mother and my sister, Rollo, had both died a few days after I had left Scotland, and that my mother's last words were: 'I now die contented and satisfied, since I know that my poor son is safe.'

My relation was one of those grammatical blockheads who thoroughly understand Latin and Greek, but who are profoundly ignorant of the human heart and of the most ordinary circumstances of life. Had he been capable of the slightest reflection, he would have prepared me for such an overwhelming blow. I remained for a moment confounded, immovable as a statue, then suddenly turned around and flew downstairs, uttering not a word in answer to his foolish compliments. When I got into the coach, I could scarcely tell the coachman to drive me home. I nearly suffocated in the coach, where I fainted and remained for some minutes insensible. I recovered from my fainting fit with a torrent of tears, which were a great relief to me. The coachman, who knew nothing of my state, continued his course, and I am even disposed to believe that the rough motion of the coach was of great benefit to me. When I reached my lodgings, my landlord, who had a kind and compassionate heart, seeing me in distress, followed me into my room and, having learned the cause of it, immediately began to moralise and repeat to me all the old and hackneyed phrases of scholastic condolence. I seized him by the shoulders in a fit of rage, pushed him rudely out of my room, and ordered him never to set foot in it again unless invited to do so. I then locked the door, threw myself on my bed, dressed as I was, and passed the night in sighs and tears, without closing my eyes.

I accused myself of having caused the death of the tenderest of mothers through the pain and anxiety she had felt for me since the battle of Culloden. I saw myself as a monster of ingratitude, having remained two months in the house of Lady Jane Douglas, within a quarter of a league of her, sick as she then was and on the point of death, without seeing her. I ought to have exposed my life a thousand times rather than not see her, in order to embrace her, bid her an eternal *adieu*, and receive her blessing. My father in his letters had concealed these deaths from me, from an apprehension that the news would be too distressing for me and in the belief that my situation was already sufficiently painful. In this, however, he acted injudiciously. By breaking the news to me gently and with precaution, he might have protected me from the danger of a shock such as I in fact experienced when it was sprung on me like a clap of thunder, a shock that might have proved fatal for me.

I had written a note to the uncle of my charming Peggy, acquainting him with the distressing news I had received, and at about ten o'clock the next morning I heard a knock on my door. I was still in the state I had been in on entering my lodgings the night before, without all my clothes on and without having even changed my attitude since throwing myself on my bed. But oh heavens, what a relief to my sufferings it was when, instead of my landlord, whom I supposed to be at my door with the intention of renewing his importunate and stupid lectures, I heard the gentle voice of my adorable Peggy, come like a guardian angel to dispel in a moment the storms and tempests by which I had been beset, and to restore to me life itself. My divine beauty had arranged this visit with her uncle, who by nature had an aversion to the society of people in distress, in order to engage me to pass the day with her. The moment I saw her I felt as though a healing balm had at once pervaded my whole frame. My suffering and agitation suddenly diminished. Viewing her, my soul became at once serene and tranquil. She entered warmly into my sufferings, sharing my distress, and the tears that fell from her lovely eyes, which I eagerly wiped away with my lips, were a thousand times more insupportable to me than my own pain and distress.

She insisted on my dining and passing the day with her. I could refuse her nothing, although I was so much disfigured from the red and swollen appearance of my eyes that an acquaintance would hardly have known me. As soon as I had changed my linen, I repaired to her uncle's, who entered very warmly into my misfortunes, and my charming Peggy did everything in her power to dissipate the sorrow and melancholy which preyed on me.

A day or two after I had treated my landlord somewhat harshly, he sent a servant to me to say that if I were visible he wished to have the honour of speaking to me. On entering my room, he made a number of excuses for having taken it upon himself to console me, observing that his heart bled on seeing me in such deep distress. He then proposed to me, by way of a party of pleasure, to accompany him to the house of a friend on Tower Hill, who had promised him a window from which he could see two rebels beheaded, the Earn of Kilmarnock and Lord Balmerino. I thanked him for his attention, but excused myself, telling him that he might easily see that I had too feeling a heart to take any pleasure in spectacles of that description. He little imagined that I was as guilty as they, and that there was no difference between us except my good fortune in having escaped being taken prisoner.

A friend came to inform me that the captain of a merchant ship, whom he knew to be a man of honour and fidelity, had undertaken, for his sake, to take me on board disguised as a sailor. In order to avail myself of this opportunity, however, it was necessary that I should embark the next morning. The idea of tearing myself away from all that was dear to me was too much, and I therefore answered that this opportunity was not without risk of discovery, for they had only to look at my hands, which were too delicate for those of a sailor, to uncover the disguise. Besides, as I knew nothing of the management of a vessel, the fiction would be perfectly plain and obvious. He obviated these difficulties by telling me that the captain of the vessel had foreseen them, and would pass me off as a sick person the moment I boarded his ship. He urged me very much to embrace this opportunity, as he ardently wished to see me out of danger. All of his arguments were, however, in vain. He could not understand how I could continue to expose myself to the danger of being beheaded on the scaffold when I had within my grasp the means of escaping this danger. Of course, he knew not that I loved my Peggy more than I loved my life.

One day, while Peggy and I were dining *tête-à-tête*, she became all at once pale, her air restless and embarrassed, and her eyes continually turned to the windows that looked into the street. She kept rising at every instant, and was incessantly leaving the room and returning. Having several times asked her, with eagerness, if anything was the matter, and whether she was unwell, she answered equivocally and in monosyllables. I earnestly entreated her to be frank with me about the cause of her uneasiness during the past quarter of an hour. 'Oh, my dear friend,' she exclaimed, 'you are undone. I see a person who is certainly an officer of justice, and I have observed him for some time passing and re-passing before our house with his eyes incessantly fixed on the door. He is undoubtedly sent to watch our house until a detachment comes to take you prisoner. Perhaps someone, having recognised you this morning and followed you to the house without you observing him, has informed against you. I have examined the house from the cellar to the garret, and there is no place where you can conceal yourself.'

I examined the man and, in reality, no police runner could have had a more villainous appearance. This development alarmed me, the more so as a person in the dress and with the appearance of a porter had, three days before, asked for me at her uncle's. As he would not say whence he had come, they had told him that I had left the house. When I had first lodged at the house of my woman friend, my former landlady, I had imprudently told her the address of Peggy's uncle, not then foreseeing the consequences. I suspected at first that the present difficulty might have its origin in a feeling of revenge on her part, as none but she could have known that I spent every day, from morning to night, in the house in question; but when I reflected on her great sweetness of temper and goodness of disposition, I could not think her capable of such baseness. I had gone out every morning in a hackney coach with the blinds up, so that it was almost impossible that I should have been recognised by anyone in the street. In short, I knew not what to think of the matter.

As the man continued to walk back and forth, never losing sight of the door of the house, I knew not what course to take. I was undecided as to whether I should go out immediately, before the arrival of the soldiers, and trust to my sword and my heels, which would create a terrible uproar in the street, or whether I should remain quietly in the house and await the result. My charming Peggy sprang to my neck and, tenderly embracing me, declared with impassioned warmth: 'No, you shall not die on the scaffold! If I cannot succeed in saving you through the interests of my friends who are in favour at court, I will visit you in prison the evening before the day of execution with two doses of poison, and I will take one to set you an example of how to make use of the other.'

The idea of my adorable Peggy's dying by poison filled me with horror, but I did not in the least doubt that she was capable of keeping her word, knowing as I did the violence and determination possessed by the fair sex in England, to a degree not found in any other nation. As for me, poison would have been, of all things, the most acceptable to me after my condemnation, and supplying me with it would have been the friendliest action.

I entreated my Peggy to examine the house with me once more. During this survey I noticed a window in the garret by which I could go out onto the roof and proceed to the roof of a neighbouring house. I immediately dispatched Peggy to watch at the window below, as a sentinel, with a silver bell in her hand, which she was to ring as soon as she saw anyone approach the door to knock. It was agreed that the ringing of the bell would serve as the signal for me to go out onto the roof. I took off my shoes lest they should make me slip on the slate and break my neck. Putting them in my pocket, I held the window with both hands, with the intention of springing out the instant I heard the bell. Having remained a quarter of an hour in this attitude, in the utmost uneasiness, my dear Peggy returned with an altered countenance, and immediately said, with a smile: 'A plague on them both. It is, I think, the sweetheart of my chambermaid. She has just asked my permission to go out for a walk, and the moment she was in the street, she familiarly took hold of his arm.'

17. Penetrating Grief

A few days after this adventure, while I was dining with Peggy and her uncle, a servant entered and informed me that a gentleman wished to speak with me in the antechamber. I immediately went out and was surprised to find Mr Colville, Lady Jane Douglas's man of business. He told me that Lady Jane had decided to live in France, and that he had been sent to London to procure a passport, which she had obtained for one servant more than she actually had, in order that she might have the opportunity of taking me with her and thus enabling me to escape to Holland. He had left her at Huntingdon, about twenty leagues north of London, in the house of a Mr Raith, where she would wait three days for me before setting out for Harwich, accompanied by Mr Stewart and Miss Hewitt.

What dreadful news! Before knowing my divine Peggy, nothing would have been so ardently wished for by me as such an opportunity to escape. But matters were now changed. I lived, and desired to live, only for my Peggy. I remained some moments quite confounded, not knowing what to answer. I was resolved not to avail myself of Lady Jane Douglas's offer, but at the same time I was embarrassed as to how I should immediately find a plausible excuse to justify my refusal, and was apprehensive lest Lady Jane should imagine, from the extravagance of my conduct, that I had lost my senses. For who would ever imagine that anyone with the prospect of execution on the scaffold in the event of his discovery, which prospect was every day before him, would refuse an opportunity to escape that danger? After a moment's reflection, I told Mr Colville that I should, during the whole course of my life, retain the most grateful sense of the goodness of Lady Jane towards me, but that, as my friends in London had discovered several means of enabling me to escape to the Continent, without any danger of discovery, I would not for the world again expose her Ladyship to any troublesome embarrassment, having already put her kindness so much to the test. I begged Mr Colville to tell her in his letter not to wait for me in Huntingdon as, when I reflected on the inconveniences and dangers to which I should thereby expose her, I could not think of availing myself of her generous and obliging offer.

Mr Colville immediately took his leave, and I returned to the table without saying a word about what had taken place. I mentioned only that it was the man of business of Lady Jane Douglas, whom she had sent to enquire after me. During the interview I had dreaded nothing so much as that the uncle, not knowing the person with whom I was in conversation, might, from uneasiness on my account, leave the dining room and join us. In that event, the discovery of my inconceivable extravagance would almost certainly have led him to suspect the true cause of my refusal.

As soon as the uncle went out, which he invariably did in the afternoon, I told my dear Peggy about the obliging offer of Lady Jane Douglas, and the difficulty I had experienced in refusing it, adding that I had done so as I would have refused any offer that would separate me from her. 'Ah, my dear friend,' she replied, 'you've done very wrong in refusing it. I suffer continuous pain and uneasiness on your account, which I conceal from you. Your situation fills me with unceasing apprehension, and hardly a night passes in which I do not dream that I see you in the hands of the executioner. As the last occasion that presented itself was not without the danger of discovery, I imagined that it might tear you from me only to bring you to immediate punishment, and I was therefore glad that you refused it. But this opportunity is very different.

Lady Jane Douglas is of so illustrious a family that the court would not dare displease her, or insult her, by subjecting her to a rigorous examination on the basis of mere suspicion. And as there could be no positive information in such a case, you would have run no risk with her. You could have effected your escape.'

I felt the most penetrating grief on hearing her persuading me to depart, and I interrupted her with accusations of inconstancy, warmly reproaching her for her indifference. 'No, my dear friend,' she exclaimed, 'you wrong me. My feelings for you are so little changed that I reserve for you a proof stronger than any you have yet received, which I had not wished to disclose until a favourable moment arose for carrying my project into execution. I have long been determined to share your fate, and to abandon for you my country, my parents, and whatever is dear to me. I have waited only for a safe opportunity for your escape without danger. Such an opportunity, long desired by me, now presents itself in the offer of Lady Jane Douglas. I will disguise myself as a man and take my passage in the same packet boat as Lady Jane, without appearing to know you. Let us go immediately in quest of clothes among the brokers, in order that we may be ready to set off tomorrow morning. Providence,' she added, 'will give us bread, and I shall be content to live with you on rustic fare, in preference to all the riches of the universe.'

I embraced my adorable Peggy with tears in my eyes, assuring her that I loved her more than life itself. I emphasised that it was that very tenderness and affection which could never allow me to plunge her into ruin and wretchedness which would, at the same time, draw down upon myself the contempt and indignation of her whole family. If I had any certainty of our being able to subsist independently of others, the case might be different, but I did not know what would become of me on reaching a foreign country, nor how I should subsist until I obtained employment. My dear friend, seeing me determined not to permit her to take this precipitous step, spoke no more of my departure. We passed that evening with the full pleasure and satisfaction that only two persons completely devoted to each other can know in such a situation.

Having returned to my lodgings after supper, I went to bed but was unable to sleep. A thousand reflections crowded my mind. I contemplated my situation in London which – independently of the danger of being arrested, to which I was continually exposed – was such that I had no certainty of being able to subsist for any length of time. Having already experienced the harshness of my father, it was evident that I should, sooner or later, be in want of money. My Peggy had the prospect of being one day very rich, but she did not, any more than myself, possess an independent income. As it was my intention, as soon as I could effect my escape, to go to Russia, where Peggy knew I had the most powerful protection through the credit of my two uncles, I flattered myself with the prospect of being able to obtain a regiment on my arrival or soon afterwards. I thus hoped for a change in my circumstances, such as would enable me to share my fortune with her. Then I could either return to England *incognito* to visit her, or induce her to come to the country where I was in service.

I also thought that as it was in the interests (in every sense of the word) of France to re-establish the house of Stuart on the throne of England, the court of Versailles might abandon the old system, on which it had acted for eighty years, of making use of this unfortunate house as a scarecrow to frighten the English, a policy now worn out and entirely unproductive, and at length make a serious attempt in favour of Prince Charles.

I should then return to England in a brilliant situation to rejoin my Peggy. A thousand other considerations made me hesitate as to whether I should avail myself of this opportunity of escaping with Lady Jane Douglas, but always on the supposition that my dear friend devoutly wished me embrace it, independently of her project of accompanying me.

I rose betimes, and went to breakfast with Peggy. As soon as her uncle had left the room to dress, I told her of my nocturnal reflections, asking at the same time her opinion and insisting that she herself would decide whether I should go or remain. She renewed her proposal of accompanying me, but I solemnly protested that I would never allow this, and that it was useless to speak any more on that subject. I would rather perish by the hand of the executioner than allow her to precipitate herself into an abyss of ruin and destruction. Seeing that I was inflexible, she told me that I decidedly must accompany Lady Jane Douglas, and that she would willingly sacrifice her own happiness and tranquillity to see me out of danger. As time was of the essence, and as I could not expect that Lady Jane would wait an instant for me at Huntingdon after hearing my answer to Mr Colville, she ordered me to go immediately to the coach office and secure a place in the diligence that travelled in one day from London to Huntingdon, which would set off at three o'clock the next morning. I forwarded my luggage at the same time so that I might have nothing on my mind to distract me from my dear Peggy. Finding her uncle in the room on my return from the coach office, I mentioned to him the offer of Lady Jane Douglas, my determination to accept it, and my intention of setting off the next morning. He expressed his satisfaction at my good fortune in finding so favourable an opportunity, although he regretted that I was so soon to quit them.

I took my leave of her uncle immediately after dinner, and

went to meet Peggy at the rendezvous we had selected, to pass the few precious moments left to us in a solitary walk out of town. That afternoon, the most melancholy we had ever known, was spent in reciprocal vows and promises of eternal fidelity and constancy. It nevertheless passed with the speed of lightning. A hundred times I was tempted to renounce my intention of departing, and I needed all the fortitude and determination of my dear Peggy to confirm me in my resolution. She accompanied me to the coach office where, having remained together until half-past eight, she called a coach and entered it more dead than alive.

I followed her coach with my eyes and when it had altogether disappeared, my resolution became weak and wavering. My first action was to run to the room assigned to me at the coach office with the intention of having my luggage carried back to my lodgings at the hairdresser's. Feeling it impossible to support a separation, I renounced the idea forever. Fortunately, however, reflection came to my aid before my luggage was taken away, and I realised that such a singular step would open the eyes of her uncle, betray us, and involve us in the most unpleasant embarrassments. I therefore returned to my room and threw myself down on the bed to await the departure of the diligence, surrendering wholly to despair and ready to sink under the load of my affliction.

If I could have foreseen that this was the last time I should ever see her, no consideration on earth would have torn me from her. Rather than leave her, I would have awaited coolly the ignominious death with which I was every day threatened.

18. Pursuing Lady Jane

The coach set off at two o'clock in the morning, and we arrived at Huntingdon at eight o'clock that night. Lady Jane had left for Harwich the previous evening, not supposing, from the answer of Mr Colville, that there was any reason to expect me there.

I took the post early the next morning, hoping to join her before her arrival at Harwich, but the wretched post horses were so fatigued by the rate at which I proceeded that I was obliged to sleep over at Newmarket. The following morning I hired a curricle, and arrived before sunset at an arm of the sea, about a league in breadth, from which I could see Harwich on the other side. A frigate of about forty guns was riding at anchor in the middle of this arm of the sea. I immediately applied to the owner of the boats and the other craft stationed there for a passage across. In spite of all my entreaties, threats and offers of rewarding him handsomely, he refused, telling me that the government had prohibited all passage after sunset on account of smuggling, and that the frigate was stationed there for the express purpose of enforcing this prohibition. I was grieved and enraged beyond measure to think that I might lose the opportunity of accompanying Lady Jane after the painful struggle I had endured in deciding whether or not to avail myself of it. But his obstinacy was not to be overcome, either by my entreaties or by my threats. He told me that the captain of the frigate, who was drinking with his officers in the owner's tavern, would throw him into prison if he complied with my request, and his vessel would be impounded as well.

The captain of the frigate, having heard my dispute with the owner of the boats, came out of the tavern to question me. I was not at all disconcerted, and answered at once that I was a servant of Mrs Gray – the travelling name Lady Jane had taken – who was now at Harwich, ready to embark in the first packet boat for Holland. I told him she had sent me to London to execute some commissions for her, and that I was uneasy lest she should leave Harwich before my arrival with an account of my dealings on her behalf. This, I said, was due to the obstinacy of the master of the boats, whom I could not induce to give me a passage, either by my offer to pay him generously or by my threat to have him punished by complaining to the governor of Harwich. I entreated the captain, with great earnestness, to make use of his authority to compel him, assuring him that I should not fail to make a faithful report to my mistress of his kindness. He told me that he had seen Mrs Gray arrive the evening before, that she appeared to be a very amiable lady, and that he should be extremely happy to have it in his power to be of any service to her, but that he could do nothing with the owner of the boats as he had received positive orders not to cross this arm of the sea after sunset. He added that Mrs Gray could not have set sail as the wind was unfavourable, and he offered to take me in his own boat and land me at Harwich as soon as he should be put on board his frigate. I did not hesitate to accept this offer, and entered his boat, not only without apprehension but boldly and eagerly, telling him that my mistress would be most grateful for his civility and kindness. I would probably have been ruined beyond remedy if I had shown the least timidity or distrust.

We were scarcely a musket-shot from the shore when the captain pointed out one of his midshipmen in the boat, by the name of Lockhart, asking whether I knew his family in Scotland. I answered in the negative, telling him that I had never been in any service other than that of Mrs Gray. I was uneasy lest Mr Lockhart should recognise me, for I had been a schoolfellow of his elder brother and had frequently visited

the house of his father, Mr Lockhart of Carnwath, and he
might therefore very possibly have known me. He was about
eighteen years of age, and had been in the navy for four years.
His eldest brother, the heir to a considerable estate, had been
foolish enough, like so many others, to join the standard of
Prince Charles.

I was privately tormented by the thought that the captain
of the frigate secretly intended, by his civility in offering me
his boat, getting me quietly on board his ship where he would
immediately make me his prisoner. Supposing that even if
young Lockhart had not known that I had been in the army of
the Prince, there was nevertheless something very mysterious
and equivocal about me being disguised in the dress of a
servant. I had no choice, however, but to submit to my destiny.

As the boat approached the ship, I began to count the
minutes that would elapse before I might be handcuffed and
ironed. My heart beat dreadfully, although I preserved a calm
exterior and answered with coolness and equanimity the
thousand questions the captain asked me, appearing not in the
least disconcerted. I nevertheless expected that at any moment
this politeness would freeze, the mask of civility falling away,
and that the sailors would be ordered to seize me by the
neck. Of all my adventures since the battle of Culloden, this
caused me the most cruel anxiety and suffering. I could not,
however, have foreseen it, nor could I have avoided it without
abandoning altogether the project of escaping to Holland
with Lady Jane. In all my other sinister encounters, there had
always been some ray of hope in the possibility of defending
myself or taking to my heels, but here I was caught like a fish
in a net. At length, on reaching the ship, the captain invited
me on board to drink a glass to the health of my mistress. I
looked on this as the denouement of the piece, and replied
that I was afraid that my mistress would have gone to bed

before my arrival in Harwich, and that I had to communicate to her some very important intelligence. He immediately put an end to my sufferings, calling out to the sailors to land me in the town, and he asked me not to forget to present his compliments to Mrs Gray.

19. The Final Crossing

I found Lady Jane Douglas at the inn, and immediately told her of my obligation to the captain of the frigate and the purgatory I had suffered during the passage. She praised my firmness, but also laughed at the singular irony of having made the officers of King George accomplices in saving a rebel who had attempted to tear the crown from the brow of their sovereign in order to place it on the head of Prince Charles.

As the wind was contrary, we remained two days at Harwich before embarking. During our stay the governor of the town, to whom Lady Jane Douglas had been recommended, became our tormentor from his excessive politeness and civility. He had received orders from London to show her every attention, and he came twenty times a day, at all hours, to ask if she had any occasion for his services. I always bolted the door of the room to prevent being surprised at table with my mistress. While we were at dinner, the governor knocked at the door but could not be admitted until I had removed my plate and the table had been re-arranged for three persons. Having opened the door to the governor, I took my station as servant behind the chair of Lady Jane, and when she asked the governor to taste her wine, I presented him with a glass. It was easy to see from his countenance that he was suspicious, but to insult a person of Lady Jane's illustrious birth without being certain of the fact might be attended with inconvenience.

The first letter I received from my beloved Peggy informed me that there was a report in London that Prince Charles had escaped to Holland with Lady Jane Douglas, disguised as her servant. There was every reason for supposing that the governor had informed the court of his suspicions, and it was fortunate for us that we had set sail the next morning, before he could receive any answer authorising him to act on his suspicions.

We arrived at Helvoetluys within twenty-four hours. During our passage, I experienced a whimsical enough scene. Sir —— Clifton, who happened to be on board the packet boat, was an acquaintance of Mr Stewart, and he was invited into the cabin Lady Jane had engaged for herself and her *suite*. His servant and I remained in a little antecabin, where we were very uncomfortably situated and a source of great annoyance to each other. This rendered us both very irritable and bad-tempered, and when we were in bed our legs continually touched each other's due to the smallness of the space in which we were cooped up. We suffered the more as there were a great many passengers on board, and the rainy weather prevented them from going on deck. The result was that this little place was always literally crammed, and it was hardly possible to breathe. Each believing the other to be a footman, our respective observations were delivered insultingly and contemptuously, and the scene would certainly have terminated unfortunately if Lady Jane had not informed the Baronet at dinner that there was a young gentleman in her *suite* who had been with Prince Charles and whom she wished to invite into her cabin to eat something. The Baronet told her that he was in a similar predicament, as the person who was acting as his valet was a Mr Carnie, an officer of the Irish brigade in the service of France. We were both invited into the cabin to dinner and, on receiving the necessary explanations, we were very much surprised and made a thousand excuses to each other for our incivility.

I was in a deep sleep when we arrived at Helvoetsluys, and all the other passengers were on shore before I was awoken. I immediately rushed out of the packet boat, my eyes still half-closed with sleep, and began to run from it as fast as I could, as though the captain and his crew had it in their power to arrest me.

I could scarcely persuade myself that I was beyond the reach of the English. Lady Jane laughed heartily at seeing me run, and called out to me that it was entirely useless, as I was now out of all danger. Only then did I thoroughly wake up.

20. Free at Last

It is impossible to express the pleasure and satisfaction I felt on finding myself safe at last, after being six months between life and death. No one, without having been in a similar situation, can have any idea of my delight at that moment. Ever since the battle of Culloden, the idea that I should end my days miserably on the scaffold had never ceased to haunt me. Now I felt, as it were, raised from the dead.

After remaining in Rotterdam for eight days, I departed with Lady Jane to the Hague, where she took up residence. As I had long determined to return to Russia, I immediately wrote to my uncle to acquaint him with the distressing situation in which I was then placed, requesting him to inform his friends, Prince Curakin and Count Gollovin, that I should be in St Petersburg in a few days, and asking him to endeavour to induce them to honour me again with their protection, that I might find some employment on my arrival. Had I followed this resolution, I should have been a general officer many years ago. I was on the point of setting out for Russia, however, when Lady Jane persuaded me to defer my departure until we had some positive news of the fate of Prince Charles.

Mr Trevor, the English resident in Holland, presented a memorial to the states-general, demanding that all Scots who had taken refuge in Holland be arrested and delivered up to the English government. To the eternal disgrace of this infamous republic, the Dutch were cowardly enough to comply with this requisition, violating both international feelings of humanity and the law of nations. There were then about twenty Scotsmen of our party in Holland. Mr Ogilvie was arrested and sent to London, and the rest turned their backs on this worthless country as fast as they could. As it was necessary that I should remain until I could find an opportunity of going to St Petersburg, I hastened to Leyden to enter myself at the university there as a student of medicine. The privileges of this university were then so extensive that the states-general could not arrest any of its students except for the crime of assassination. Having succeeded in obtaining the insertion of my name in the register of students, by means of a few ducats paid to Professor Gaubeus, I returned immediately to the Hague, where we learned a few days later that Prince Charles had escaped to France. My desire to see him again and the hope of another attempt in his favour made me abandon my decision to go to Russia, and my fate was decided for the rest of my days by my arrival in Paris towards the end of the year 1746.

ALSO FROM THE HOUSE OF EMSLIE –

Edward Carson QC

by

Edward Marjoribanks

'The author's account of Carson's
cases makes riveting reading for
lawyer and general reader alike.'

– SIR SYDNEY KENTRIDGE QC

This brilliantly written book will fascinate all lawyers, inspire
law students and those contemplating a legal career, and
interest all who appreciate well written biography and Anglo-
Irish history.

Distributed in the United Kingdom by Central Books
99 Wallis Road   London   E9 5LN
Tel: 0208 986 5463   Fax: 0208 533 5821

Also available as an e-book
www.twitter.com/houseofemslie

ALSO FROM THE HOUSE OF EMSLIE –

Commando
Of Horses and Men

by

Deneys Reitz

'Reitz had the uncanny knack of living through the war as though leafing through the pages of an adventure story.'

– Thomas Pakenham

Commando, Deneys Reitz's brilliantly told story of hardship and adventure, is widely regarded as the classic autobiographical account of the Anglo-Boer War. A bestseller since its publication in London in 1929, it has never been out of print. This edition, subtitled *Of Horses and Men* (the author's working title), relates the story of Reitz's exile in Madagascar, a poignant yet humorous account of struggle in the aftermath of war.

Distributed in the United Kingdom by Central Books
99 Wallis Road   London   E9 5LN
Tel: 0208 986 5463   Fax: 0208 533 5821

Also available as an e-book
www.twitter.com/houseofemslie

ALSO FROM THE HOUSE OF EMSLIE –

Trekking On
in the company of brave men

by

Deneys Reitz

'I had forgotten what a fluent storyteller Reitz
was, and what wonderful stories he had to tell.'

– DR J DE V GRAAFF

The compelling quality of this book lies in the fact that the
daredevil adventurer who seems to have almost courted disaster
during 'the war to end all wars' was also a gifted writer with an
eye for detail, a complete absence of rancor, and an insight,
tinged with dry humour, that transcended national differences.

Distributed in the United Kingdom by Central Books
99 Wallis Road   London   E9 5LN
Tel: 0208 986 5463   Fax: 0208 533 5821

Also available as an e-book
www.twitter.com/houseofemslie

CAPE REBEL

STORIES   VOICES   PLACES

'All autobiography is storytelling, all writing is autobiography.'
– J M Coetzee

Stories by and about gifted storytellers, voices that continue to shape our lives, places that spark our imaginations – these lie at the heart of the Cape Rebel, where almost everything we do has a story attached.

We admire truth, courage, integrity and humour, wherever they are found.

If you share our interest in storytelling that makes you smile, think or question, and that inspires what is best in the human spirit –

Go to www.caperebel.com and join us to receive our concise weekly email.

We'll never share your information, & you can unsubscribe with a single click at any time.

www.caperebel.com